Contents

Family Secrets

About the Workbook

Note to Parents

This workbook is for your kids. It's also for you, in a different way.

The questions are designed to *unlock your child's emotions*, to get them thinking and writing about what they feel. Many children of divorce bottle up their worries, resentments, and self-doubt. In a nonthreatening way, this workbook can urge them to open up and guide them in doing so.

Because of that possibility, this workbook can also *get you and your kids talking about stuff*. You know what I mean by "stuff": all those things it's too hard to talk about. Why did you break up? What will happen to me? Is it all right for me to still love Daddy (or Mommy)? Tough questions. But you have to get them out in the open, or they'll stagnate and poison your child's heart. Warning: There may be some things that are hard for you to hear. But even these difficult matters can draw you and your child closer together.

This workbook will also *tell your kids they are not alone*. Millions of children have been touched by divorce, and we've talked with hundreds of them. Their comments, printed here, can reassure your child. "Hey, that's exactly how I feel." There's comfort in that.

Comfort also comes from God. This workbook will *try to get your kids talking to God*. Relax—we're not pushing them into a particular doctrinal system. But we do teach that God loves them and cares for them, even in tough times. Many children—and adults— have found strength in God as they deal with the aftereffects of divorce.

Finally, this book will *help your kids choose positive behavior*. We deal with "family secrets" and try to show the young reader how to break these dysfunctional cycles. Some might say this is too complicated for children, but we've explained it in simple terms—and we feel it is essential for kids to know.

Note to Facilitators

It is imperative that an adult facilitator go through this workbook with the child. Preferably this person is someone who already has built a relationship with the child and who knows a little bit about the child's family situation. Possibilities include parents, stepparents, other family members, significant others, teachers, guidance counselors, pastors, youth pastors, Sunday school teachers, support group leaders. The child is the one who actually interacts with the workbook; the adult's role is to facilitate this process through encouragement, active listening, and appropriate intervention.

Each chapter begins with *Action Steps.* Here you will find the goal and objectives for the child, steps to work through the material, and ideas for further topic discussion. Your job is to facilitate the process of interaction between the child and the workbook, not to teach the material. Our goal is learning—not through the process of passed-on knowledge, but through the process of personal experience.

The purpose of this workbook is to change lives by touching children where they hurt. If children can get in touch with and express their feelings about their parents' separation or divorce, they have a better chance of avoiding problems later in life related to their parents' separation or divorce. Our hope is that this workbook will be a tool to help kids break the cycle of divorce and dysfunction. You are a valuable part of this process: a caring, adult friend who will listen to the pain and will guide the child toward healing that pain.

How to Use This Workbook

You may use this material in several ways. Two of the best approaches are as follows:

▶ **Read the material to the child.** This works best with younger children. Set aside a special time to read the material, bit by bit, with your child. Since the workbook involves activities, bedtime is probably not best. Because the issues here are so weighty, a schedule of once or twice a week might be better than daily. That will give some breathing (and mulling) time between sessions.

Your child may need private time to do the activities. For instance, the letters to God, to yourself, and to the other parent may require some personal thought. Give your child time alone to work on these but be ready to talk about it.

▶ **Check up on the child's reading.** This works best for eleven- and twelve-year-olds. Let your child go through the workbook at his or her own pace but check up on the progress every week. Go through it with your child. Ask what he or she learned. See if you need to discuss any issues.

This workbook has grown out of a divorce recovery program for children ages 7–12 called Fresh Start for Kids. This program is sponsored by Fresh Start Seminars, Inc., an organization working with the separated and divorced throughout the country via radio, seminars, and publications. Fresh Start for Kids provides programs for children of divorce that include seminars, retreats, camps, support groups, and counseling. We'd be happy to send you information about any of our programs or publications.

Gary A. Sprague, ACSW
Fresh Start for Kids

Fresh Start Seminars, Inc.
63 Chestnut Road
Paoli, PA 19301

1-800-882-2799

Action Steps for the Introduction

GOAL FOR THE CHILD

- To understand your family

OBJECTIVES FOR THE CHILD

- To learn about the three kinds of families
- To learn about the three kinds of brothers and sisters
- To learn what kind of family you live in
- To learn what kinds of brothers and sisters you have
- To draw your family

STEPS

- Child fills in name, age, grade, and family situation
- Facilitator explains the three kinds of families
- Child fills in the kind of family she lives in
- Facilitator explains the three kinds of siblings
- Child fills in the kind of siblings he has
- Child draws family
- Child explains drawing

IDEAS

- Ask child to show you photographs/videos of her family.
- Allow child to make own decision about who to include and who not to include in the family drawing. This tells you how he feels about each member of the family.
- Tell child that other kids live in the same situation.
- Assure child that one family situation is not necessarily better than another. The strength of a family depends on what happens in the family, rather than on who is in that family.

Introduction

My first name is _____.

My last name is _____.

I am _____ years old. I am in the _____ grade.

Fill in the blanks that apply to your family situation:

I was _____ years old when my parents separated.

I was _____ years old when my parents divorced.

I was _____ years old when my mom died.

I was _____ years old when my dad died.

I was _____ years old when my mom married my stepdad.

I was _____ years old when my dad married my stepmom.

There are three kinds of families:

► Birth families have two birth parents (see figure I. 1).

► Single-parent families have only one parent (see figure I. 2).

► Blended families have two parents; one is your birth parent, one is your stepparent (see figure I. 3).

Answer the following questions:

Do you live in a _____ single-parent or a _____ blended family?

Do you live with your _____ mom or your _____ dad?

How often do you visit your mom? _____

How often do you visit your dad? _____

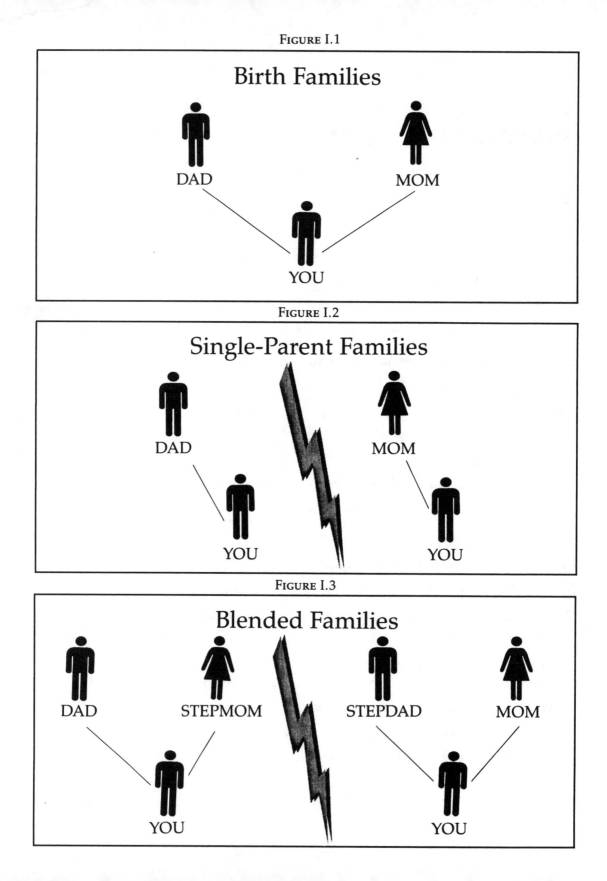

FIGURE I.1

Birth Families

DAD

MOM

YOU

FIGURE I.2

Single-Parent Families

DAD

YOU

MOM

YOU

FIGURE I.3

Blended Families

DAD

STEPMOM

STEPDAD

MOM

YOU

YOU

There are three kinds of brothers and sisters:

▶ For birth brothers and sisters, both parents are the same (see figure I.4).

▶ For half brothers and sisters, one parent is the same, and one parent is different (see figure I.5).

▶ For stepbrothers and stepsisters, both parents are different (see figure I.6).

Tell about your brothers and sisters:

Name	Age	Birth	Half	Step
____	____	____	____	____
____	____	____	____	____
____	____	____	____	____
____	____	____	____	____
____	____	____	____	____
____	____	____	____	____
____	____	____	____	____
____	____	____	____	____
____	____	____	____	____
____	____	____	____	____

My Family Scene

Draw your family.

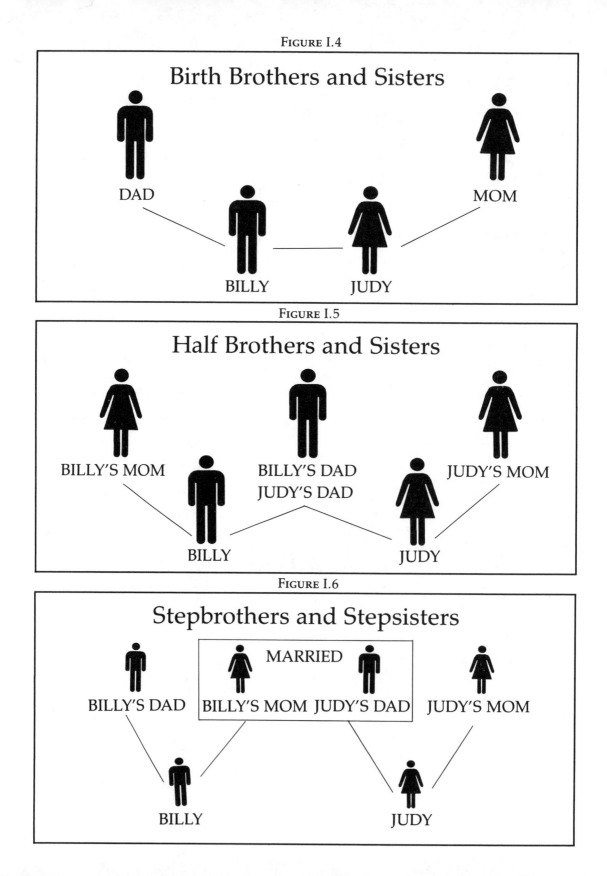

FIGURE I.4

Birth Brothers and Sisters

DAD BILLY JUDY MOM

FIGURE I.5

Half Brothers and Sisters

BILLY'S MOM BILLY'S DAD JUDY'S DAD JUDY'S MOM BILLY JUDY

FIGURE I.6

Stepbrothers and Stepsisters

MARRIED

BILLY'S DAD BILLY'S MOM JUDY'S DAD JUDY'S MOM BILLY JUDY

How It Feels

In this section we are going to talk about the feelings that you might have as a result of your parents' being divorced or separated. You will learn about feeling bad, sad, mad, and maybe even glad. You will also learn about feeling shocked, afraid, and confused.

In this section you will learn that your parents' divorce was not your fault and that you are not the only one who has divorced parents.

If you talk about how you feel because of your parents' getting divorced, you will feel better about it. You will also have a better chance of avoiding problems in the future.

Please take your time when you do each activity so you will have a chance to think about how it feels.

Action Steps for Chapter 1

GOAL FOR THE CHILD
- To understand how you feel about your parents' divorce or separation

OBJECTIVES FOR THE CHILD
- To learn about feeling bad
- To learn about feeling sad
- To learn about feeling mad
- To learn about feeling glad
- To draw your feelings

STEPS
- Facilitator or child reads quotes at beginning of chapter
- Child fills in answers to questions about feelings
- Facilitator or child reads definitions of feelings
- Child circles how he feels about the divorce/separation
- Child draws a picture describing how he feels
- Child explains drawing to facilitator

IDEAS
- Make sure that child understands the definitions of feelings.
- Give the child freedom to express his feelings.
- Do not make value judgments about the child's feelings.
- Help the child learn how to solve problems when dealing with conflicts.
- Encourage the child to talk to the people with whom he is angry.
- Give the child time to explore how he feels.

Chapter 1

Feeling Bad, Sad, Mad, and Glad

I feel sad that my parents broke up.   Iva, *Age 10*

I felt bad. I also felt depressed. You never know what will happen.   Bobby, *Age 8*

I didn't really care because they were fighting a lot anyway.   Craig, *Age 9*

I felt sad, afraid, helpless, and scared.   Candice, *Age 11*

I felt shocked, mad, lonely, and worried.   Deron, *Age 10*

I feel mad because my dad lies a lot.   Joy, *Age 9*

I was very upset and depressed. I punched a wall and hurt my hand.   Cameron, *Age 12*

I felt glad because my dad always fought with my mom.   Ronesia, *Age 11*

Make It Your Own

What things do you do when you feel bad?

_____

_____

_____

_____

What things do you do when you feel sad?

_____

_____

_____

_____

What things do you do when you feel mad?

_____

_____

_____

_____

_____

What things do you do when you feel glad?

_____

_____

_____

_____

▶ The dictionary defines feeling **bad** as suffering pain or distress.

When you feel bad about the divorce, it is usually because seeing your parents split up is painful. It is like a hurt that is deep inside where nobody can see it. It is up to you to tell someone that you feel bad so that person can help you feel better.

▶ The dictionary defines feeling **sad** as grief or unhappiness.

When you are sad that your parents got divorced, it is okay to cry. You are very unhappy. Sad feelings take time to heal. Don't try to make believe that your parents' divorce doesn't bother you because you will only feel worse if you do. It is okay to feel sad.

▶ The dictionary defines feeling **mad** as carried away by intense anger.

When you feel mad at your parents, you need to talk to them. Sometimes it is good to cool down first, but it will make you feel better if you tell them why you are angry. If you keep your anger inside, you will probably get a stomachache. Don't take your anger out on somebody else by getting into a fight either, because that will only make matters worse. Hit a pillow and then go talk to the one you are angry at, and see if you can solve the problem.

> *When you feel mad at your parents, you need to talk to them. Sometimes it is good to cool down first, but it will make you feel better if you tell them why you are angry.*

▶ The dictionary defines feeling **glad** as feeling pleased or delighted.

If you are happy that your parents got divorced, it is probably because one of your parents was mean and hurt you or another family member. Some parents drink too much, take drugs, say mean things, or touch their children in ways that are not right.

Maybe the parent that left was never home anyway, so it hardly seems like anything is different. Maybe you are afraid to admit that you feel bad, sad, or mad, so you tell everyone that you feel glad instead.

You are okay no matter what you are feeling. You are not bad, even if you feel bad. You will truly be glad if you can say how you really feel—even if that means feeling bad, sad, or mad.

> *You are okay no matter what you are feeling.*

Make It Your Own

How do you feel about your parents' divorce or separation? (Circle words that apply.)

ANGRY	CONFUSED	DEPRESSED	EXCITED
AFRAID	GLAD	GRIEVED	GUILTY
HAPPY	HELPLESS	HOPELESS	LONELY
LOST	LOVED	MAD	REJECTED
SAD	SCARED	SHOCKED	WORRIED

Draw a picture that describes how you feel.

Action Steps for Chapter 2

GOAL FOR THE CHILD

- To understand how you feel about your parents' divorce or separation

OBJECTIVES FOR THE CHILD

- To learn about feeling shock
- To learn about feeling fear
- To learn about feeling confusion
- To understand the things that you worry about

STEPS

- Facilitator or child reads quotes at beginning of chapter
- Child fills in answers to questions about feelings
- Facilitator or child reads definitions of feelings
- Child checks the things that she worries about
- Child shares why she checked particular items

IDEAS

- Make sure child understands the definitions of feelings.
- Help the child understand what is happening to her.
- Help the child develop action steps to overcome worry.
- Encourage the child to ask specific questions of parents.
- Avoid giving the child "pat" answers to erase the worry.
- Try to increase your own tolerance for unanswered questions.

Chapter 2

Shock, Fear, and Confusion Too

I was afraid because my dad fought with my mom.   Curtis, *Age 8*

Divorce is confusing, very confusing.   Rhoyce, *Age 9*

I felt shocked when my parents divorced.   Allyson, *Age 10*

I don't understand why they are not together.   Jeff, *Age 7*

The one thing I always thought was strange was that I didn't feel any pain then or after they told me. The only time I felt pain was when people teased me. It took a few days to sink in. I didn't even believe I had wakened when I got up and my father wasn't banging pots and pans in the kitchen. Everything was boring. There was no creativity or happiness in anything.   Charles, *Age 12*

Make It Your Own

What things do you do when you feel shocked?

_____

_____

_____

_____

_____

_____

What things do you do when you feel afraid?

_____

_____

_____

_____

_____

_____

_____

What things do you do when you feel confused?

_____

_____

_____

_____

_____

_____

▶ The dictionary defines **shock** as a sudden disturbance or surprise.

When you first find out that your parents are splitting up you can hardly believe it. You are used to everybody's being together and can't even think about what it would be like if your parents lived separately. You say to yourself, "I can't believe that this is happening to me!"

> *You say to yourself, "I can't believe that this is happening to me!"*

If you continue to act like nothing has happened, you are probably refusing to accept the fact that something has gone wrong. You might not want to face it, but you must accept the fact that your parents have made a decision to split up. You will have to start making adjustments to your new and different family.

▶ The dictionary defines **fear** as unpleasant anticipation of danger.

Often you feel afraid about what is going to happen to you now that your parents are getting divorced; it is pretty scary. You might ask questions like these: Where am I going to live? Who is going to take care of me? Will I have to move? Will my family have enough money now? All of these concerns are normal, and it is very important to talk to both of your parents about these things. Ask as many questions as you need to. Your parents can comfort you if you are afraid. Going to see the new home of the parent that leaves might help. Remember that you will be taken care of, and you don't have to worry about your basic needs. Your parents should be able to take care of you even though they are living in two different places now.

Where am I going to live? Who is going to take care of me? Will I have to move? Will my family have enough money now?

▶ The dictionary defines **confusion** as being disordered or mixed up.

It gets very confusing when parents get divorced. You never seem to be able to figure things out. You wish someone would tell you what is going on. Sometimes parents explain things to you differently or give you two different reasons why something has happened, and you don't know who to believe. The only way to clear up the confusion is to ask your parents to tell you the truth. It takes time to clear up confusion, so be patient with your parents as they try to explain things to you in ways that you will understand (and also in ways that won't make the other parent look bad).

The only way to clear up the confusion is to ask your parents to tell you the truth.

Make It Your Own

Which of these things do you worry about?

- ☐ Who will take care of me?
- ☐ Is there anybody that I can count on?
- ☐ Where are my parents going to be living now?
- ☐ Will my parents stop loving me too?
- ☐ Is my parents' divorce my fault?
- ☐ Are there other kids who have divorced parents?
- ☐ Can I get my parents back together again?
- ☐ Will my parents get sick or worse?

- ☐ Will we have enough money now?
- ☐ Will I have to move to a new neighborhood?
- ☐ Will I have to change schools?
- ☐ Will I have to meet new friends?
- ☐ Are my parents going to remarry?
- ☐ Whom will I live with if my parents remarry?
- ☐ Will my parents fight over custody of me?

What other things do you worry about?

_____

_____

_____

_____

_____

_____

Action Steps for Chapter 3

GOAL FOR THE CHILD
- To understand that your parents' divorce or separation is not your fault

OBJECTIVES FOR THE CHILD
- To learn common reasons why parents divorce or separate
- To understand why you think your parents got divorced or separated

STEPS
- Facilitator or child reads quotes at beginning of chapter
- Child checks the reasons she thinks her parents divorced or separated
- Child discusses the items checked
- Facilitator or child reads "How Russell Got His Red Bike"
- Child answers questions about "Russell"
- Both discuss the child's answers to questions about "Russell"

IDEAS
- Do not be afraid to tell the child the real reasons for the divorce or separation, even if it involves talking about abuse, addiction, adultery, or abandonment (see the section "Family Secrets" in this workbook). Kids need to know that it was not their fault. Honesty is best!
- Tell them only the facts when talking about the reasons for the divorce or separation. Specific details are unnecessary.
- Avoid blaming one parent or the other.
- Try to share what each parent did right and wrong.
- Give the child freedom to love both parents: Do not make it impossible for the child to have a healthy relationship with both parents.
- Encourage the child to forgive her parents for what they have done wrong.
- Encourage the child to thank her parents for the things that they have done right.

Chapter 3

It Isn't My Fault!

My parents have explained to me that it wasn't my fault, but sometimes I feel that it is. I think I'm getting very confused about what is happening in my life.   Rena, *Age 9*

I used to think it was my fault that my parents got divorced. But it wasn't. It was something that went wrong in my parents' marriage.   Tyler, *Age 10*

I knew it wasn't my fault because in school there are three other kids including me. We have a divorce class, and we talk about it.   Lance, *Age 8*

I thought it was my fault because they would fight about if my room was clean and fight about things I did wrong.   Cynthia, *Age 8*

I thought that they got divorced because of me and my brothers and sister.   Hugh, *Age 7*

I don't think it was my fault because I didn't even know what was going on, and they weren't even fighting about me.   Jaimey, *Age 9*

It was not my fault because they kept fighting, and I was only three years old.   Grace, *Age 8*

It isn't my fault because I'm just a kid!   Patrick, *Age 8*

Make It Your Own

For what reason(s) do you think your parents divorced or separated?

☐ They stopped loving each other.

☐ They just could not get along anymore.

☐ They got into too many fights.

☐ They didn't know how to talk to each other.

☐ They had money problems.

☐ They changed and became very different.

☐ They were pretending to be married to someone else.

☐ They said mean things and hurt each other.

- [ ] They physically hurt someone in the family.
- [ ] They drank too much or took drugs.
- [ ] They got arrested and went to jail.
- [ ] They got sick and went to the hospital.
- [ ] They left the family and moved away.
- [ ] They slept in separate bedrooms.
- [ ] They touched their kids in ways that were not right.

For what other reasons do you think they divorced or separated?

_____

_____

_____

_____

_____

HOW RUSSELL GOT HIS RED BIKE
(with training wheels)

by Gregg Miner and Thomas Whiteman, Ph.D.

Russell and his friends, Michael and Tommy, were digging in the dirt for treasures and neat stuff. "Let's go ride our bikes down the big hill," said Michael.

"Okay," said Tommy.

"Wait a minute, guys. I don't have a bike yet," said Russell.

"Well, you better get one soon. Come on, Tommy, let's go," said Michael.

As the two boys rode away on their shiny bikes, Russell felt sad. He was a little boy who lived in a town called Boothwyn. He loved to run and play and dig in the dirt, but more than anything, he wanted his very own bike with training wheels.

One day at breakfast his Mom said, "Russ, how would you like to go to the mall with me this morning? Maybe we can have lunch at McDonald's."

"Can we look at the bikes, too? Ones with training wheels," said Russell excitedly.

"Sure," she grinned.

That day Russell had a great time. They went to several stores and saw many bikes. There were green ones, blue ones, and even purple ones, but Russell decided he liked the red one best. "Hey Mom, this one fits real good. Can we get it today?"

Mrs. Brown looked sad as she said, "Not today, Russell, but I'll talk to your dad and see how soon we can get the money. Maybe in a few weeks. Okay?"

"Okay, Mom," said Russell.

On the way home, he had a cheeseburger and fries at McDonald's. After dinner that night Russell sat looking through a big catalogue and saw just the bike he wanted. He rushed into the kitchen and shouted, "Look, Mommy and Daddy, I found just the bike I want."

His mom seemed all upset as she snapped, "Mommy and Daddy are talking right now. Please go to your room and play." Russell went in and sat on the stairs.

"It's not fair to yell at me when I didn't even do anything wrong," Russell cried. As he sat there, Russell could hear his parents yelling in the kitchen.

"You just don't understand, do you? I only make so much money. Maybe I should move out, and you can find someone who can afford to buy bikes and toys, and all the stuff you really want."

"They're fighting because of me and my bike," panicked Russell. "Daddy's going to move out!"

Without hesitating a moment Russell tore up his picture of the red bike. "What," he thought, "is going to happen to me now?"

The next day in his kindergarten class, Russell felt really sad. Mrs. Jensen, his teacher, was telling an exciting story about a wild horse. Russell was not listening. He wasn't even thinking about red bikes. He was thinking about his mom and dad. A tear came to his eye.

He felt so sad that even the teacher noticed. "What's wrong, Russell?" asked Mrs. Jensen. She was worried too, and so she called Russell's mom.

"Hello, Mrs. Brown? This is Rita Jensen, Russell's teacher. Russell is really upset about something. I just wanted to let you know—is anything wrong at home that's bothering him?"

Mrs. Brown sighed, "His dad is moving out next week. Russell must have overheard us arguing." She paused a moment and then said in a trembling voice, "Thanks for calling me."

That night after dinner Russell's dad called him into the kitchen. "Russell, your mom and I want to talk to you about something very important. Sometimes when moms and dads live together for a while they have a hard time getting along. Sometimes they decide it's best to live apart—at least for a while. Now Russell, you know your mom and I fight a lot. We decided it would be best if . . . if I move to another apartment for a while."

"Oh, Daddy, don't do that. I don't want the bike anymore. You can use the money from it to pay bills and stuff," cried Russell.

Russell's dad was surprised. "Russell, this is not your fault in any way. It has nothing to do with your bicycle either."

"We both love you very much," said Mrs. Brown in a trembling voice. "This problem is just between your daddy and me."

"But when I showed you the bike I wanted, you yelled, and when I was gone Daddy said, 'I'll leave so you can afford to buy stuff you want,'" said Russell sadly.

"Russell, sometimes when moms and dads are angry we say things that don't come out right, but that is just because we are mad," explained Mr. Brown. "Daddy loves you very much." Mr. and Mrs. Brown both reached over and gave Russell a hug.

"As a matter of fact, Russell, I'm going to live just a few minutes away, and you can see me a lot," said Mr. Brown. "We talked it over, and since your birthday is coming soon we decided to get you a red bike."

And that's how Russell got his new bike with training wheels. Mr. and Mrs. Brown are still living in different places, but Russell knows that it is not his fault and that they both love him very much. He visits his dad on his new red bike, and now he doesn't even need training wheels.

Make It Your Own

Did you ever feel the way Russell did—thinking it was your fault when your mom or dad decided to leave?

_____

In the story, Russell was angry and scared when he heard that his dad was leaving. How did you feel when you first learned that your mom and dad would be breaking up?

_____

_____

_____

_____

_____

Russell had a very difficult time listening in class when he found out that his dad was leaving. Do you find yourself thinking about problems at home when you're supposed to be listening in class or doing your homework?

_____

Russell's parents split up because they fought a lot. Why did your parents split up?

_____

_____

_____

_____

_____

At the end of the story, Russell felt both good and bad feelings. He was sad that his parents were no longer together, but he was happy that he could go to visit his dad on his new red bike. Do you feel these same kinds of mixed feelings?

_____

What are some of the things that make you sad?

_____

_____

What are some of the things that make you happy?

_____

_____

What are some of the good things about your parents' breakup?

_____

_____

Action Steps for Chapter 4

GOAL FOR THE CHILD

- To understand that you are not the only one who has parents who are divorced or separated

OBJECTIVES FOR THE CHILD

- To identify other kids who have parents that are divorced or separated
- To plan to talk to other kids who have parents that are divorced or separated
- To learn about support groups
- To learn about journals
- To learn how God can be the strength in your life

STEPS

- Facilitator or child reads about support groups and journals
- Facilitator discusses possible support groups
- Child completes box activity and applies what he learns
- Facilitator or child reads "The Case of the Midnight Scream"
- Child answers questions following the story
- Facilitator and child discuss answers
- Facilitator or child reads the Bible verses
- Child answers related questions and writes in journal
- Child finds feelings in the word search puzzle

IDEAS

- Help the child find a support group to join.
- Help the child begin a journal on a regular basis.
- Explain that the child can make choices that will help him feel better about his parents' divorce or separation.
- Encourage child to let God be the strength in his life.

I Am Not Alone!

You have read comments at the beginning of Chapters 1, 2, and 3 written by kids like yourself who have parents that are either separated or divorced. You need to know that you are not alone! You are not the only one who has parents that are separated or divorced. You are also not alone in what you are feeling. Other kids are feeling the same things that you are.

> *You are not the only one who has parents that are separated or divorced.*

Support Groups

So that you don't feel alone, join a group with other kids who have parents that are separated or divorced. Your school, church, or community center might offer such a group. These groups usually are called support groups for children of divorce.

Journals

Another thing that can help you is to start a journal. A journal is a book that you write in. You write your thoughts and feelings down on paper. You can do this every day or whenever you would like. Adults write in journals. Kids can write in journals too! Nobody will see your journal unless you show it to them.

> *A journal is a book that you write in. You write your thoughts and feelings down on paper.*

Start a journal in a separate notebook, and write in it often. You may be surprised at how good you feel after you write down your thoughts and feelings. In addition, we will give you a chance to write in a personal journal at the end of each section. We hope you find this activity helpful too.

Make It Your Own

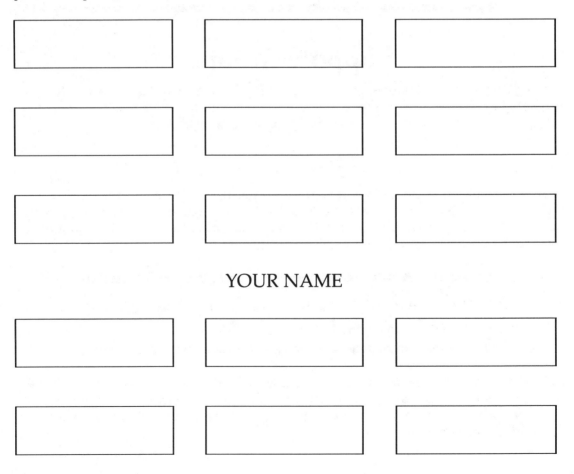 Write your name in the box in the middle of the page.

In the boxes surrounding your name, write the names of kids that you know who have parents that are separated or divorced.

Color in two of the boxes of kids you would like to talk to about what you have in common.

Invite the kids that you have colored in over to your house to talk to them about your parents' separation or divorce.

When you finish this activity, you will realize that you are not alone. Try to talk with these friends about your feelings, and see if they have similar feelings about their parents' separation or divorce.

YOUR NAME

THE CASE OF THE MIDNIGHT SCREAM

by Gregg Miner and Thomas Whiteman, Ph.D.

"Mom, . . . Mom, . . . Can you help me? Mom! I'm stuck. Hurry up please!" screamed Russell.

"Okay, okay, I'm coming," said Mrs. Brown, as she hurried up the stairs. "Russell, I told you that you can't wear that camouflage army shirt camping. It doesn't fit you anymore. Well, no wonder you can't get it off. You've got that big knife in your hand. Why don't you put the camping knife down? Then it will be a little easier to take your shirt off," exclaimed Mrs. Brown.

"But Mom, I like to hold it," said Russell, feeling a little embarrassed.

"I know that," replied his mother, "but no one's going to steal it while you put on your shirt."

Russell's dad had given him the knife for Christmas. It was a camping knife with a fork, spoon, and two blades. Mr. Brown had promised to take Russell camping as soon as the weather got warmer. But when spring came, Mr. and Mrs. Brown separated, and Mr. Brown moved into an apartment on the other side of town.

Now Russell was going to go camping just with his mom and his sister. He was a little worried that Mom *really* didn't know how to camp and fish the right way. But he didn't want to hurt her feelings, so he didn't say anything about that.

"Can't Daddy come with us just when we go camping?" Russell asked.

"Now Russell, I explained to you that wouldn't work out," said Mrs. Brown.

"Well, I'm glad that we can go, but I still wish Daddy could too. Why did he have to move to that dumb apartment? If I was real good, would Daddy move back home?" asked Russell.

Cindy, Russell's sister, had just come in from the hallway. "Yeah, I could be better too, Mom," she said.

"Now come on, you two. We told you before. Our problems have nothing to do with you. We *both* love you very much. Please don't blame yourselves for Mommy and Daddy's fighting and breaking up. It just isn't your fault! Okay?" insisted Mrs. Brown.

"Okay, Mom," said Cindy and Russell as they went downstairs to play in the living room.

Mrs. Brown felt sad as she watched her two children. She loved both very much and did not want them to blame themselves for the breakup. "Does Russell have the idea that he is the only kid in the world with these problems? He probably doesn't want any school friends to know his dad lives in a separate apartment," she thought.

"Dear God, please help Russell and Cindy know that they are not alone, and that many kids have separated or divorced parents," she prayed aloud.

Suddenly the doorbell rang. "It must be Mrs. Collins and Donny," yelled Russell.

Mrs. Brown was going to be watching Donny to make extra money. Also she hoped Donny would be good company for Russell.

Excited, Russell yanked open the door; then stood there in shock. "Not *that* Donald," he thought. Russell remembered this Donald Collins. "He's the creep from kindergarten who always made fun of me. I wish I could tell his mom about the ladybug he stuck in my ear." In horror he suddenly realized, "He's going to find out Mommy and Daddy are broken up! What am I gonna do now? I just *know* he'll make fun of me."

"Well, hello. You must be Russell," said the tall lady standing in the doorway. "Your mom has told me so much about you and your sister Cindy. You and Donald are going to have so much fun camping this weekend. I wish I could go."

"Hello, Mrs. Collins, come on in," said Russell, gaining his self-control.

As Donald walked in, he said, "Hi, Russell."

"Hi, Donny. Wanna see my camping knife?" said Russell, adding quickly, "My dad can't go camping. He has to work."

"Yeah, mine too," replied Donny without looking at Russell.

After Donald's mom left, they had lunch. Then Mrs. Brown and the kids packed the car and way before dark they reached the campground.

"Hey, guys, this sure is a neat place," exclaimed Donny.

"Yeah, our dad told us about this place. He knows all about camping," said Russell.

Mrs. Brown came over and said, "I'm going to start dinner."

"Can I help, Mom?" asked Cindy.

"Sure," responded Mrs. Brown. "Boys, I want you to see if you can put up the tent. If you have any problems, call me for help."

"Don't worry, Mrs. Brown," said Donny. "We can do that. My daddy showed me how when we went camping last month."

"Show-off!" thought Russell. It was soon clear that Donny would be the boss.

"I'll stand in here and hold up the pole; you drive in the stakes," Donny ordered.

Russell did as Donny said, but the tent kept falling over.

"Oh, I remember now. I'll hold up the tent till you get the stakes in," said Donny, somewhat confused. Maybe Mrs. Brown was the only one who knew anything about putting up a tent.

Russell felt like he was doing all the work, but he stretched the ropes and drove in the stakes anyway.

"Okay, it's all up now," said Russell when he had driven in the last stake.

"Hey, where's the door?" said Donny. Russell started laughing. The tent looked like a large sack with a cat inside fighting to get out. "Help me find it, Russell," cried Donny. There *was* no door!

"What a dumb tent—no doorway," said Cindy.

Mrs. Brown said with a grin, "Pull up the stakes, Russell. You scouts set the tent upside down and the door is facing the ground."

With Mrs. Brown's help they raised the tent the right way.

Russell felt better during dinner. Donny, and even Cindy, kept looking at the camping knife his dad had given him. Its shiny, sharp blade gleamed in the firelight. Russell cut sticks like they were paper and carved all kinds of fancy swirls. Donny seemed impressed.

Russell felt even better when Mr. Show–off Donny tripped on a root and dropped his beans and hot dog in the dirt. As he went down, beans landed like spitballs on the ground all around. Maybe Donny wasn't such a "big shot" after all.

"Now if I can just keep him from finding out Mommy and Daddy are separated!" thought Russell. The problem was that blabbermouth Cindy might mention it at any time.

That night Cindy and Mrs. Brown slept in the van while Donny and Russell bedded down in the tent.

"Man, this is great," thought Russell. "I'm really having fun now, and I don't even miss Dad." Neither boy had a problem going to sleep either. Both were still as logs when suddenly—probably about midnight—both were startled awake. Way off in the distance, they heard a horrible scream. "Someone is yelling for help—he's in trouble," cried Donny.

"No, he's not yelling, he's screaming *hard*!" Russell looked at Donny whose eyes were as big as fried eggs. Russell was so scared that he was shaking all over, and his heart was pounding. The scream, and then a crashing sound, grew louder and louder.

"What if he comes in here," he thought. The crashing through the bushes grew louder and closer too.

"He's going to hit the tent!" whispered Donny.

Gradually, the screaming and clattering died down, and the two boys heard a huge splash in the lake. Then there was silence. The boys waited for a long time. Neither dared to speak. The man—whoever he was—was gone. All they heard was croaking frogs and chirping crickets.

"Why didn't your mom and Cindy hear that noise?" squeaked Donny.

"I dunno," replied Russell shakily. "I guess they were tired and had the windows up in the van because of the mosquitoes."

"Why don't you g-go get your mom?" whispered Donny. But Russell didn't move except for the shaking; neither did Donny. After a long time of silence, both boys fell asleep.

Late the next morning, Russell jerked awake when he felt a cold, wet hand grab him by the throat. He yelled, and right next to him Donny yelled too. Russell jumped up still in his undershorts until he realized that Cindy was in the doorway—laughing. Then he noticed that in Donny's hand sat a warty green frog.

Cindy was giggling and jumping around like popcorn. She tripped over a stick and fell, but just lay there laughing and laughing. Russell was so mad that he wanted to scream. "Cindy, you creep! I'm telling Mom!" said Russell. Then both he and Donny remembered at the same time—the scream at midnight!

In two seconds the boys had on their shoes and were both jabbering at once to Mrs. Brown about the mysterious scream at midnight.

"I didn't hear anything. Are you sure?" she asked. "Okay, okay, I'm convinced. You obviously believe it really happened."

"After breakfast we'll go solve this mystery," she said.

The boys chewed and gobbled really fast and waited in frustration for the girls to get ready.

"You three get started, and I'll catch up," said Russell's mom.

"Yeah, let's go. This is neat!" said Cindy. "A real mystery!"

"No, that's okay, we'll wait," Donny responded uneasily.

"Hmm, these kids are genuinely scared," thought Mrs. Brown.

While the boys waited, Russell said, "Man, if my dad could have come, he would know just what to do. He's the . . ." He stopped right in the middle of his sentence. Donny was crying. "What's the matter, Donny?"

"I don't have a dad like you do. My parents divorced a long time ago, and I haven't seen my dad since I was four years old, and I miss him, especially now," cried Donny.

"Oh," said Russell. He was too surprised to think of what to say.

"Okay, detectives," called Mrs. Brown. "Let's go solve this mystery!"

For a moment, neither boy moved. Russell realized Donny felt bad, thinking about his dad. "Donny is like me because I feel bad too."

"Let's go," Mrs. Brown said again.

"Oh, my goodness, Mommy! Look over here," yelled Cindy who was ten steps ahead of the rest.

Cindy pointed to a path of broken ferns and trampled bushes. Mrs. Brown was amazed. Even long, thorny bushes were bent and broken. The trail of destruction crossed right over their path and kept on going. "How strange—must have been a big animal," she said.

"No, he was a man. We could tell," said both boys at once.

"Yeah, the man screamed, 'Oh no,' and then he said a bad word, and started yelling some more and crashing through the bushes," Russell explained.

"Look over here," said Donny and Cindy at the same time. There in a soft spot was a foot mark—a big footprint, unmistakably human. They followed the trail of footprints, which were visible in the muddy places, until they found a muddy sneaker.

"Oh dear, this *is* strange," said Mrs. Brown.

Continuing, they traced the trail through the bushes. Russell carried the sneaker. Occasionally, they spotted more footprints where the ground was soft. Finally, the trail led down to the beach and into the water.

"That guy was flying," said Donny. "Look how far apart these footprints are!"

"Yeah!" said everyone else.

"Well, kids, that's the end of this trail," said Mrs. Brown, who didn't feel very much like camping anymore. "Let's go back to the campsite. We'll get the car and drive over to the ranger's station to talk to someone about this."

All the way to the ranger's station Donny and Cindy didn't stop talking for one second, but Russell couldn't get out of his mind what Donny had said: "My mom and dad are divorced." When he thought about it, he had tears in his eyes. Russell felt that he wanted to say something to encourage Donny.

Suddenly, he realized the car was stopping as he slammed into the back of the front seat.

Mrs. Brown said, "Come on, everyone, let's get some answers." Russell thought it kind of made it scary to realize his mother was taking their mystery so seriously.

The park ranger had a light brown shirt and hat with a hard rim just like a state policeman.

"Hello, ma'am. I'm Bill Evans. Can I help you?" said the ranger.

"Well, Mr. Evans, we're up on campsite 101, and we would like to report some strange things happening."

With that as an introduction, all three kids began talking at once, explaining about the thrashing in the bushes, the screaming, and the tracks that disappeared into the water. When they had finished, Mrs. Brown said, "Well, that's about it, Mr. Evans. Has anyone else reported any of this to you?"

"As a matter of fact," Mr. Evans answered, "there is a man in the hospital right now who I think is your mystery man. You see, he is a fisherman who wanted to get a jump on the fish, so he decided to go down in the dark and catch a few."

"That's illegal, right?" asked Cindy.

"Well, not really. But anyway, on the way to the lake he stepped on a hornets' nest. He really got them stirred up. They started chasing him. The faster he ran, the faster they came. He was stung many times, and the only way he could get rid of them was to jump into the lake and go underwater. Eventually he swam to shore and contacted us to take him to the hospital. I suspect if you look somewhere near your campsite, you'll find a discarded fishing rod and a sneaker stuck in the mud."

"We found the sneaker," said Cindy.

By the time they left Ranger Evans, it was time to break camp and go home.

"What a great first camping trip!" said Donny, as he and Russell were walking down the path to wash up before going home.

"Yeah, it sure was. We could write our very own mystery novel with this story," said Russell. "But you know, Donny, I need to tell you something. You know when I said my dad had to work? Well, he did, but the real reason he didn't go with us was because my mom and dad are breaking up, and I think they are getting divorced, just like your mom and dad."

Donny stared at Russell for a while, and then finally said, "Really? I didn't think I knew any other kids with that problem."

"Yeah," said Russell, "it really stinks, doesn't it?"

"It sure does," responded Donny. "You know, Russell, I'm glad we went camping together. Let's you and me be best friends."

"It's a deal. Let's shake on it," said Russell.

"What are you guys doing now? It's time to go. Mom says hurry up. We've got a long drive home," yelled Cindy.

And that ended "The Case of the Midnight Scream."

But that did not end Donny's and Russell's friendship. They are even better friends now. They can talk to each other about their dads' being gone and what it's like to live with just their moms. It was good for them to learn that they are not the only ones whose parents do not live together.

Make It Your Own

Do you ever feel the way Russell did; like you are one of the only ones whose parents are separated or divorced?

_____

Are you ever afraid that if others find out about your family they will make fun of you?

_____

Have you ever had to do something with your mom that you thought would be better to do with your dad—like camping and fishing?

_____

Have you met some new friends like Donny, who come from families like yours? Who are they?

_____

_____

_____

How or where do you think you could meet other friends who have family situations like yours?

_____

_____

_____

_____

If you have brothers or sisters, do you ever talk to them about your feelings about the family? Think about ways you can talk to your mother about your feelings, or perhaps your father.

_____

_____

_____

_____

WHAT THE BIBLE SAYS

The Lord is my strength and my shield;
My heart trusts in Him, and I am helped. (Ps. 28:7 NAS)

God is our refuge and strength,
A very present help in trouble. (Ps. 46:1 NAS)

[The Lord] gives strength to the weary,
And to him who lacks might He increases power. . . .
[T]hose who wait for the Lord will gain new strength;
They will mount up with wings like eagles,
They will run and not get tired,
They will walk and not become weary. (Isa. 40:29, 31 NAS)

Make It Your Own

Is God the strength of your life?_____

In what ways has God helped you with your feelings?

_____

_____

_____

In what ways do you keep God from being your strength?

_____

_____

_____

In what areas of your life do you need God's strength right now?

_____

_____

_____

My Personal Journal

_____

_____

_____

_____

_____

_____

_____

_____

_____

_____

_____

Feelings

```
O  L  S  Y  T  P  W  B  H  A  P  P  Y  C  S
S  O  A  M  F  S  E  K  R  I  K  C  F  O  R
M  N  D  K  H  Q  S  H  O  C  K  E  D  N  G
P  E  A  L  X  A  Y  E  G  N  Y  Z  D  F  U
I  L  G  A  F  R  A  I  D  D  V  H  P  U  I
Y  Y  I  S  S  P  J  Z  E  E  E  O  D  S  L
G  Y  V  C  Y  O  U  U  C  P  E  P  F  E  T
G  B  N  A  V  D  V  H  M  R  O  E  Y  D  Y
L  M  O  R  V  A  L  E  S  E  L  L  L  E  S
A  D  D  E  A  R  H  L  Q  S  O  E  J  L  Y
D  L  R  D  N  G  Q  P  O  S  V  S  A  K  X
T  R  X  F  G  N  X  L  R  E  E  S  W  I  F
U  V  L  V  R  Y  C  E  X  D  D  G  K  K  J
M  Y  B  F  Y  U  A  S  L  O  S  T  A  I  K
L  H  T  B  X  P  G  S  I  S  G  V  B  A  R
```

Find the following words in the puzzle. They are hidden vertically and horizontally.

AFRAID	ANGRY	CONFUSED	DEPRESSED
GLAD	GUILTY	HAPPY	HELPLESS
HOPELESS	LONELY	LOST	LOVED
SAD	SCARED	SHOCKED	

Things That Change

In the following chapters, you will learn about the things that change when your parents separate or divorce. Children of divorce have to adjust to many changes when their parents split up.

Four changes we are going to talk about are these:

▶ Living in a single-parent family

▶ Having both parents work

▶ Moving into a different (and usually smaller) living situation

▶ Visiting the parent who doesn't live with you anymore

You need to see how these changes in your family, finances, housing, school, friends, and relationships will affect your life. Take your time as you move through these changes. If you rush through them, it will only increase the time that it takes you to adjust to the changes.

Ask your parents to be patient with you, to support you, and to listen to how you feel about all these changes. Let them know that sometimes you just have to be upset. Your world has been turned upside down! They may want to push you to get on with life as if nothing has really happened. But you need some time to deal with the things that change.

Action Steps for Chapter 5

GOAL FOR THE CHILD

- To understand how you feel about living in a single-parent family

OBJECTIVES FOR THE CHILD

- To learn about the changes that have happened in your family
- To understand how one-parent and two-parent families are the same
- To understand how one-parent and two-parent families are different
- To talk about the things that make you feel scared and alone
- To talk about the things that make you feel safe and secure
- To draw a picture about your mom or dad's leaving home
- To learn common concerns of single-parent families

STEPS

- Facilitator or child reads opening narrative
- Child answers questions
- Facilitator and child discuss the answers to questions
- Ask child to draw a picture showing what she remembers about Mom or Dad's leaving home
- Ask child to explain drawing to you
- Child checks concerns that she has in her family
- Facilitator and child discuss the checked items

IDEAS

- Ask child to draw a picture of how she feels about living in a single-parent family if the child was too young to remember what it was like when Mom or Dad left home.
- Ask child to interact with the material in this chapter by sharing what she remembers from living in a single-parent family if the child lives in a blended family now.
- Don't let the child throw up a smoke screen by telling you that the activities do not relate to her situation. Be creative and adjust the activities to fit the child's present situation.
- Assure the child that one family situation is not necessarily better than another.

Chapter 5

My Mom and Dad Live in Different Places

Losing your baseball in your neighbors' bushes is a drag. Losing one of your favorite toys is also pretty lousy. Losing a parent is the worst! When your parents separate or divorce and one of them moves out, you have feelings of loss. You miss the parent who doesn't live with you anymore. You have many questions about where that parent will live and when you will see him or her next. You get mad at the parent who still lives with you because you see her or him more. You have more chores and responsibilities now that you are a single-parent family.

Being a single-parent family is hard to adjust to. There used to be two parents around, but now there is only one. It is helpful to think about how families with one parent and families with two parents are the same and also how they are different. In this chapter, we will give you a chance to do that. We will also help you to understand how you feel about living in a single-parent family and to take steps toward adjusting to all these changes in your family.

Make It Your Own

What things in your family have changed now that your parents live in different places?

_____

_____

_____

_____

How is your family similar to or different from a family with parents who live together?

_____

_____

_____

_____

What have you missed most about your parents' not living together? _____

_____

_____

_____

_____

How did you respond to the news that your parents were separating or getting divorced?

_____

_____

_____

_____

What did other people do to try to make you feel better about the loss? _____

_____

_____

_____

What things in your family have stayed the same since your parents separated or got a divorce?

_____

_____

_____

Is it okay to cry? _____

Does it make you feel better to cry? _____

What things make you feel scared? _____

_____

_____

_____

What things make you feel alone? _____

_____

_____

_____

What things make you feel safe? _____

_____

_____

_____

What things make you feel secure? _____

_____

_____

_____

Why is it hard to talk to your parents about your feelings? _____

_____

_____

_____

When does the hurt stop? _____

_____

_____

_____

My Family Scene

Draw a picture that shows what you remember about your mom or dad leaving home.

Make It Your Own

Which are concerns that you have in your family?

- ☐ I feel different from kids living in two-parent families.
- ☐ I am jealous of my friends living in two-parent families.
- ☐ I am embarrassed that my parents live in different places.
- ☐ Both of my parents have to work now.
- ☐ There's never enough money to buy things.
- ☐ I come home to an empty house after school.
- ☐ I have extra responsibilities and chores now.
- ☐ We don't have enough room where we now live.
- ☐ I wish I could spend more time with my parents.
- ☐ My parents are too tired to give me quality time.
- ☐ I wish my parents would get back together again.
- ☐ I worry that the parent I live with will leave me too.
- ☐ It is hard to talk to my parents.
- ☐ I don't feel safe or secure in my family anymore.
- ☐ My parents fight about the visitation arrangements.

What other concerns does your family have?

_____

_____

_____

_____

_____

_____

Actions Steps for Chapter 6

GOAL FOR THE CHILD

- To understand how you feel about both of your parents working

OBJECTIVES FOR THE CHILD

- To talk about what your family was like when only one parent worked
- To talk about what your family is like now that both parents work
- To draw a picture about having both parents working

STEPS

- Facilitator or child reads opening narrative
- Child answers questions in left column
- Facilitator and child discuss the answers to questions
- Child answers questions in right column
- Facilitator and child discuss the answers to questions
- Child circles feelings about having both parents working
- Facilitator and child discuss items that the child circled
- Child draws a picture showing how she feels about both parents working
- Child explains drawing

IDEAS

- Ask child to talk about changes that have taken place in the quantity or quality of time spent with Mom and Dad, if both of the child's parents work.
- Talk about latchkey issues: coming home from school to an empty house, going to a baby-sitter's or day-care center before or after school, helping out with extra chores and extra responsibilities, growing up too fast.
- Bring up the fact that there is not as much money now as before. Ask child to talk about how the divorce or separation has affected what she needs to buy or wants to buy.

Chapter 6

Both of My Parents Work Now

Before your parents separated or divorced, you lived with both of your parents. Now that they are living in different places, chances are that both of your parents are working. This might be the same as it was before, or it may be a big change for you and your family. There are many changes that you are having to adjust to as a result of both parents' working.

Some of these changes might be: seeing both of your parents less, not having as much money to buy things as you did before, coming home from school to an empty house, going to a baby-sitter or day-care center before or after school, and helping out with extra chores because now there are two homes to keep up. In this chapter, we will give you a chance to understand how you feel about having both of your parents working and help you talk about the best ways to make adjustments to these changes.

Make It Your Own

When only one parent worked

What jobs did you do in your family?

_____

_____

_____

_____

What was it like when you came home from school?

_____

_____

_____

Now that both parents work

What jobs do you do in your family now?

_____

_____

_____

_____

What is it like when you come home from school now?

_____

_____

_____

What was dinner like?

_____

_____

_____

_____

What things did your family spend money on?

_____

_____

_____

_____

What is dinner like now?

_____

_____

_____

_____

What things does your family spend money on now?

_____

_____

_____

_____

How do you feel about having both parents working? (Circle all that apply.)

ANGRY	CONFUSED	DEPRESSED	EXCITED
AFRAID	GLAD	GRIEVED	GUILTY
HAPPY	HELPLESS	HOPELESS	LONELY
LOST	LOVED	MAD	REJECTED
SAD	SCARED	SHOCKED	WORRIED

My Family Scene

Draw a scene (or cartoon) showing how you feel about having both parents working.

Action Steps for Chapter 7

GOAL FOR THE CHILD
- To understand how you feel about moving into a different living situation

OBJECTIVES FOR THE CHILD
- To talk about your old house and your new house
- To talk about your old neighborhood and your new neighborhood
- To talk about your old school and your new school
- To talk about your old friends and your new friends
- To write a letter to your friends in your old neighborhood
- To draw pictures of your houses, neighborhoods, schools, and friends

STEPS
- Facilitator or child reads quotes at beginning of chapter
- Child writes down what he remembers most and draws a picture of the old house, old neighborhood, and old school
- Child writes down what he remembers most and writes a letter to a friend in the old neighborhood
- Facilitator discusses these memories with the child
- Child writes down what he likes most and draws a picture of the new house, new neighborhood, new school, and new friends
- Facilitator discusses these new experiences with the child

IDEAS
- Try not to rush the child into feeling good about making all these changes. Give child time to make the proper adjustments.
- Give the child the opportunity to express his feelings of loss about the old house, neighborhood, school, and friends.
- Encourage the child to look at these new experiences in a positive way.
- Ask the child to talk about what life would be like if he has to move in the future.

Chapter 7

New Friends and New Schools

I am sad because my parents live in separate houses, and it is not fair for the kids.   Gina, *Age 9*

We are living with my mom's best friend.   Lonnie, *Age 7*

I sort of liked moving because I met more friends.   Bernita, *Age 8*

I would be scared to move. And it would be hard to make friends.   Latrell, *Age 8*

I had to move four times, but I enjoyed it. I changed schools four times, but I was not nervous.   Erin, *Age 10*

My dad moved, and he took all the new furniture that was in the den. I was very, very mad.   Marvin, *Age 10*

I felt bad when my dad moved because I thought that I would never see him again. I do get to see him every week now. It is very hard to live with no dad in the house. He told me someday that I could live with him.   Jonathan, *Age 11*

I moved right after my parents separated. I was five years old. When we moved my mom didn't like our new house. After a few years my mom decided to move again. We moved into a big house, but my mom couldn't afford it unless she went to work. So she went to work. I really miss her. I wish she didn't have to work.   Mitzy, *Age 12*

Make It Your Own

My Old House

What do you remember most about your old house?

_____

_____

_____

_____

_____

_____

_____

_____

Draw a picture of your old house.

My Old Neighborhood

What do you remember most about your old neighborhood?

_____

_____

_____

_____

_____

_____

_____

_____

Draw a picture of your old neighborhood.

My Old School

What do you remember most about your old school?

_____

_____

_____

_____

_____

_____

_____

Draw a picture of your old school.

My Old Friends

What do you remember most about your old neighborhood friends?

_____

_____

_____

_____

_____

_____

_____

Write a letter to a friend in your old neighborhood.

_____

_____

_____

_____

_____

_____

_____

_____

_____

_____

My New House

What do you like most about your new house?

_____
_____
_____
_____
_____
_____
_____

Draw a picture of your new house.

My New Neighborhood

What do you like most about your new neighborhood?

_____
_____
_____
_____
_____
_____

Draw a picture of your new neighborhood.

My New School

What do you like most about your new school?

_____

_____

_____

_____

_____

_____

_____

_____

Draw a picture of your new school.

My New Friends

What do you like most about your new friends?

_____

_____

_____

_____

_____

_____

_____

_____

Draw a picture of your new friends.

Action Steps for Chapter 8

GOAL FOR THE CHILD

- To understand how you feel about visiting the parent that doesn't live with you anymore

OBJECTIVES FOR THE CHILD

- To talk about the things you like about visiting your parent
- To talk about what you don't like about visiting your parent
- To draw a picture about visiting your parent
- To learn about ways that we can count on God

STEPS

- Facilitator or child reads quotes at beginning of chapter
- Child completes the visitation agreement activity
- Facilitator and child discuss the visitation agreement
- Child draws a picture describing what she enjoys doing with the parent that she visits
- Child explains drawing to facilitator
- Facilitator or child reads the Bible verses
- Child answers related questions and writes in journal
- Child finds changes in the word search puzzle

IDEAS

- Encourage child to talk with her parents about the details of the actual (legal) visitation agreement and to say what she likes and dislikes about it. Changes can be made if all parties consent.
- Stress communication between both parents and children as the key to having a successful visitation plan. If the child wants to visit more or less, she needs to tell parents.
- Encourage child to tell parents what she likes and dislikes doing during the visits. Most kids would like to spend *time* with the parents instead of receiving gifts, watching TV or competing for the parents' attention.
- Encourage child to count on God to always be there.

Chapter 8

I Visit Them Every Other Weekend

I am sad because I only see my dad once a month. I wish that I could see him every weekend.   Alysia, *Age 9*

I like to visit my dad in Chicago. He is moving to Tampa, Florida, so I won't be going to Chicago anymore.   Franky, *Age 8*

I feel good when I see my dad because it is fun going places with him. I love him, and I want my dad and mom to forgive me. He is very nice. He never hurts me. He said he would never hurt me.   Emma, *Age 10*

When I visit my dad, he takes me to wrestling. I like that.   Bo, *Age 7*

I don't visit my dad. He lives in California. My dad is mean like other mean men.   Marla, *Age 8*

Every day after school I ride home to my dad's house. After work, my mom comes to pick me up.   Sam, *Age 10*

I visit my dad every other weekend. He doesn't do that much with me. It's not very fun. My sister doesn't play with me. Sometimes we go places together.   Taneka, *Age 9*

We get to visit my dad every other weekend and some weekdays. When I am mad at my mom it makes me glad, but when I am mad at my dad it makes me mad.   Vernell, *Age 9*

Make It Your Own

Pretend that you are the judge who set up the visitation agreement between you and your parents. Write down the details to this agreement and then show it to your parents. Although this may not change anything because this agreement is not legal, it will be a way of telling your parents how you feel about visitation.

Visitation Agreement

Child's name _____

Child would like to live with mother _____ days per week.

Child would like to live with father _____ days per week.

Child would like to live with _____ _____ days per week.

Child would like to do the following activities with mother:

1. _____

2. _____

3. _____

4. _____

Child would like to do the following activities with father:

1. _____

2. _____

3. _____

4. _____

Child does not enjoy the following activities with mother:

1. _____

2. _____

3. _____

Child does not enjoy the following activities with father:

1. _____

2. _____

3. _____

My Family Scene

Draw a cartoon or picture that describes what you enjoy doing with the parent that you go to visit.

WHAT THE BIBLE SAYS

You can be sure that God will be with you always and continue with you until the end of the world. (Matt. 28:20 NCV)

God has said, "I will never leave you; I will never forget you." So we can feel sure and say, "I will not be afraid because the Lord is my helper. People can't do anything to me." (Heb. 13:5, 6 NCV)

Make It Your Own

Can you count on God to always be there? _____

In what ways have you been able to count on God? _____

_____

_____

In what ways are you running away from God? _____

_____

_____

In what areas of your life do you need to be close to God?

_____

_____

My Personal Journal

Changes

```
E  P  W  P  I  W  H  H  V  D  A  T  I  N  G
L  U  N  P  C  F  C  H  O  R  E  S  P  V  S
B  S  E  P  B  E  X  F  A  M  I  L  Y  V  B
K  R  C  V  A  E  M  J  Y  Z  P  Z  C  G  B
W  O  R  K  R  L  V  I  H  J  V  V  Y  E  C
R  Y  X  F  H  I  J  E  R  Z  I  V  N  M  E
H  O  M  E  F  N  F  P  D  G  S  Q  N  P  X
P  V  I  I  R  G  W  A  G  F  I  U  U  T  E
U  G  T  P  I  S  C  P  U  A  T  E  M  Y  R
B  S  I  E  E  V  B  E  O  T  S  S  O  H  U
C  K  M  O  N  O  T  F  C  H  R  T  N  O  S
I  L  E  V  D  Z  U  K  H  E  H  I  E  U  H
J  C  F  J  S  K  X  X  F  R  A  O  Y  S  B
X  J  Y  M  O  T  H  E  R  N  M  N  D  E  X
S  C  H  O  O  L  I  D  Y  F  K  S  C  B  V
```

Find the following words in the puzzle above. They are hidden vertically and horizontally.

CHORES	DATING	EMPTYHOUSE	FAMILY
FATHER	FEELINGS	FRIENDS	HOME
MONEY	MOTHER	QUESTIONS	SCHOOL
TIME	VISITS	WORK	

New Family Relationships

In this section you will learn about the new family relationships that start when your parents divorce.

The first things that change are your relationships with your mother and with your father. During these changes, try to forgive them for thoughtless ways they may act.

The next thing that changes is that your parents may start dating. Your mom may have a boyfriend now. Your dad may have a girlfriend. Try not to compare your mom with your dad's girlfriend or to compare your dad with your mom's boyfriend. Try to avoid thinking that this new person is taking the place of one of your parents.

Another change might take place if your parents remarry. This creates a lot of changes including stepparents, stepbrothers and sisters, and half brothers and sisters. Allow enough time to build these relationships so that you feel comfortable with these new people who become family members.

No matter how many new parents or new siblings you now have, remember that nobody can take the place of your birth parents. Life will seem complicated at first. Soon you will find that good can come from these new family relationships.

Action Steps for Chapter 9

GOAL FOR THE CHILD
- To understand how you feel about your parents' dating

OBJECTIVES FOR THE CHILD
- To talk about the changes in your relationship with your mom
- To talk about the changes in your relationship with your dad
- To talk about how you feel about your mom's dating
- To talk about how you feel about your dad's dating
- To write a letter to your mom
- To write a letter to your dad

STEPS
- Facilitator or child reads quotes at beginning of chapter
- Child answers questions about the relationship with Mom and with Dad before the divorce/separation
- Child answers questions about the relationship with Mom and with Dad after the divorce/separation
- Facilitator and child discuss how these relationships have changed as a result of the divorce/separation
- Child answers questions about Mom's dating, and then writes a letter to Mom
- Child answers questions about Dad's dating, and then writes a letter to Dad
- Facilitator discusses the child's answers to the questions about parents' dating

IDEAS
- Encourage the child to give the letters directly to his parents if he feels comfortable doing so.
- Do not force the child to let you read the letter or force the child to give it to his parents. Just writing the letter will help the child get in touch with feelings.
- Remember not to place value judgments on either parent. Stay neutral so the child does not have to choose sides.
- Encourage the child not to compare his parents' dating partners with actual parents.
- Encourage the child to avoid thinking that this new person is taking the place of one of his parents. If this new person becomes a family member through remarriage, the child will have to adjust to this change, but nobody can take the place of a child's birth parents.

Chapter 9

My Mom Has a Boyfriend; Dad Has a Girlfriend Too

My mom left us to go live with her boyfriend. I don't like my mom's boyfriend because he stole my mom.   Nicki, *Age 9*

If they start dating it's gonna be weird. It seems like they would be together all the time. But if they date, it might be neat because he might play with me. My real dad is disabled.   Rankin, *Age 11*

I like my dad's girlfriend. She is neat and is nice to me.   Mary, *Age 8*

I will feel mad if my mom starts to date. I wouldn't like the person. Maybe if I liked my baby-sitter, I would let Mommy go out, and then I could like the person she is dating.   Sheila, *Age 10*

My dad has a girlfriend. My mom doesn't like my dad's girlfriend. She is very nice to me, and she works at a nursing home. She lets me go there with her. My dad and his girlfriend live together.   Belinda, *Age 12*

When the baby-sitter comes, it makes me feel upset. My sister is happy when the baby-sitter comes because she likes to make up games.   Lou, *Age 10*

I don't want my mom to date because somebody that I don't really know would be always bossing me and my mom around. The reason why I don't want my mom to date is because the person might be dorky—in my words.   Mack, *Age 11*

My mom dates two different guys. I like them both. I enjoy seeing my mom date. Sometimes I go on dates with them. It is fun too.   Karen, *Age 10*

Make It Your Own

BEFORE YOUR PARENTS' DIVORCE
What were the best parts about your relationship with your mom?

_____

_____

_____

_____

_____

What were the worst parts about your relationship with your mom?

_____

_____

_____

Rate your relationship with Mom:

| 1 | 2 | 3 | 4 | 5 | 6 | 7 | 8 | 9 | 1 0 |

What were the best parts about your relationship with your dad?

_____

_____

_____

What were the worst parts about your relationship with your dad?

_____

_____

_____

Rate your relationship with Dad:

| 1 | 2 | 3 | 4 | 5 | 6 | 7 | 8 | 9 | 1 0 |

AFTER YOUR PARENTS' DIVORCE

How has your relationship with your mom changed for the better?

_____

_____

_____

How has your relationship with your mom changed for the worse?

_____

_____

_____

Rate your relationship with your mom now:

| 1 | 2 | 3 | 4 | 5 | 6 | 7 | 8 | 9 | 1 0 |

How has your relationship with your dad changed for the better?

_____

_____

_____

How has your relationship with your dad changed for the worse?

_____

_____

_____

Rate your relationship with Dad now:

| 1 | 2 | 3 | 4 | 5 | 6 | 7 | 8 | 9 | 1 0 |

Answer the following questions:

	Yes	No	I don't know
Do you want your mom to start dating?	☐	☐	☐
Should your mom tell you whom she is dating?	☐	☐	☐
Do you like your mom's boyfriend?	☐	☐	☐
Should your mom keep you from seeing your dad?	☐	☐	☐
Do you want your mom to get married again?	☐	☐	☐
Has your mom's boyfriend taken your place?	☐	☐	☐
Do you get along with your mom's boyfriend's kids?	☐	☐	☐
Do you get along with your stepdad?	☐	☐	☐
Does your mom know how you feel about this?	☐	☐	☐
Do you get along with your stepbrothers and sisters?	☐	☐	☐
Do you get along with your half brothers and sisters?	☐	☐	☐
Will your parents' divorce affect your own dating?	☐	☐	☐
Will your parents' divorce affect your own marriage?	☐	☐	☐

Write a letter to your mom. Tell her how you feel about the separation, the divorce, the idea of her dating, your stepdad, your new family members, and your relationship with her.

Dear Mom,

_____

_____

_____

_____

_____

_____

_____

_____

_____

_____

_____

_____

_____

_____

_____

_____

Answer the following questions:

	Yes	No	I don't know
Do you want your dad to start dating?	☐	☐	☐
Should your dad tell you whom he is dating?	☐	☐	☐
Do you like your dad's girlfriend?	☐	☐	☐
Should your dad keep you from seeing your mom?	☐	☐	☐
Do you want your dad to get married again?	☐	☐	☐
Has your dad's girlfriend taken your place?	☐	☐	☐
Do you get along with your dad's girlfriend's kids?	☐	☐	☐
Do you get along with your stepmom?	☐	☐	☐
Does your dad know how you feel about this?	☐	☐	☐
Will you be a better parent than your parents were?	☐	☐	☐

Will you learn from your parents' mistakes?	☐	☐	☐
Will you repeat the things your parents did right?	☐	☐	☐

Write a letter to your dad. Tell him how you feel about the separation, the divorce, the idea of him dating, your stepmom, your new family members, and your relationship with him.

Dear Dad,

_____

_____

_____

_____

_____

_____

_____

_____

_____

_____

_____

_____

_____

_____

_____

_____

_____

_____

_____

Action Steps for Chapter 10

GOAL FOR THE CHILD
- To understand how you feel about living in a blended family

OBJECTIVES FOR THE CHILD
- To learn about the changes that have happened in your family
- To talk about your stepparents, stepbrothers/sisters, and half brothers/sisters
- To learn about common concerns of blended families
- To forgive your parents for things they have done that hurt you

STEPS
- Facilitator or child reads quotes at beginning of chapter
- Child answers questions about the blended family
- Facilitator and child discuss the answers to questions
- Child checks the concerns she has in her family
- Facilitator and child discuss the items that the child checked
- Facilitator or child reads story "I Have Three Dads"
- Facilitator or child reads the Bible verses
- Child answers the related questions and writes in journal
- Child finds forgiveness in the word search puzzle

IDEAS
- Encourage the parents of the child to allow enough time for the child to build relationships with these new people becoming family members. If they have already become family members, give the child time to feel comfortable and get adjusted to these changes.
- Encourage the child not to make comparisons between stepparents and birth parents. This comparison harms the adjustment process.
- Encourage the stepparents to take on the role of stepparent, not birth parent. They will have greater success with their stepchildren if they allow them to continue healthy relationships with their birth parents.
- Allow forgiveness to heal all the wounds. Kids need to forgive parents. Parents need to forgive each other. Bitterness, unresolved anger, and slander will not help anyone. Encourage parents to model kindness and compassion even to those who are not kind or compassionate to them.

Chapter 10

New Parents and New Siblings

My mom is getting married. He is really good to me. He buys me a lot of things. He just moved in. He has no kids. I wish my mom would have more kids. They are getting married in May. So far, I'm not going to the wedding. I'm so confused about everything. I wish everything would work out with a snap.   Art, *Age 11*

I don't like my stepdad very much. He smokes, yells, and sets a bad example for me.   Scott, *Age 10*

I don't have a stepfamily. But I do have half sisters. One is twenty-one, and the other is nineteen. I like them a lot.   Sara, *Age 11*

I hope I will have stepsisters. I think that it would be fun to have stepsisters.   Jill, *Age 9*

I don't want a stepfamily because they are mean, and I hate them.   Morris, *Age 8*

My stepmom is nice. I like her a lot. She plays with me. My stepbrother is very silly. He is okay. I like my stepsister. We go shopping together.   Melony, *Age 10*

Make It Your Own

What things have changed in your family now that your parents have remarried?

_____

_____

_____

_____

How is your family similar or different from a family with parents who have not divorced and remarried?

_____

_____

_____

Why do you think kids compare their stepparents to their birth parents? Do you do the same thing?

_____

_____

_____

Why do you think stepparents try so hard to get their stepkids to like them? Does your stepparent do this too?

_____

_____

_____

How did you respond to the news that your parents were getting married to someone else?

_____

_____

_____

_____

Which concerns do you have in your family?
- ☐ I keep comparing my stepparent to my birth parent.
- ☐ I can't get along very well with my stepparent.
- ☐ I can't get along very well with my stepbrothers/sisters.
- ☐ I am jealous of my new half brother/sister.
- ☐ I feel sorry for the parent who is still single.
- ☐ My stepparent plays favorites with her own children.
- ☐ I spend less time now with my birth parent.
- ☐ I am jealous of my stepparent.
- ☐ My parents continue to put me in the middle.
- ☐ My parents are too busy to spend time with me.

☐ My stepparent competes with my birth parent.

☐ I don't know what to call my stepparent.

☐ My parent's last name is different from mine.

☐ I don't feel safe or secure in my family anymore.

☐ My parents fight about the visitation arrangements.

What other concerns does your family have?

_____

_____

_____

_____

_____

I HAVE THREE DADS

by Gary Sprague

When I was born, I met my first dad. He was my birth father and he and my mom were trying to work out their problems again. You see, my parents were separated before I was even born. They were fighting and having problems and decided to separate for a while to have some time to think about whether they should get a divorce or get back together again.

> *You see, my parents were separated before I was even born.*

My dad called my grandmother (my mom's mom) and asked her to talk to my mom about coming back home to work things out. He said that he was willing to make some changes and try to get along better with my mom. My grandmother talked to my mom, and she agreed to come back home.

My two older brothers were four and five years old at the time. I was not even a twinkle in my father's eye yet (ask your parents what that means). After my parents got back together again, my mom got pregnant with me. I guess you could say that if it wasn't for my grandmother's talking my parents into "one more chance," that I would not be here today.

When I turned three years old, my dad got transferred, and we moved from New Jersey to Chicago. This move was hard on my mom because she left all of her friends back in New Jersey and didn't know anybody in Chicago. It was probably a little bit hard on my dad too, but he was busy at work so he probably didn't think about it too much.

After a while, my parents started fighting and having problems again. When I was five years old, my parents got a divorce. It was not a surprise to anyone. I didn't cry or get angry or get scared or anything. My parents tried really hard to not let me feel anything uncomfortable about the divorce. They pretended that nothing bad had happened and moved ahead with their lives, denying the pain.

This is when I met my second dad. He was the neighbor who lived across the street. He was getting a divorce just like my mom was. His wife and four kids were moving to Florida. My mom and my neighbor got friendly and started dating. After they were both divorced, they decided to get married. I was the ring boy in the wedding. My neighbor then became my stepfather. My first dad moved out, and my second dad moved in. Everybody was happy and there was still no pain.

> *My first dad moved out, and my second dad moved in.*

I guess my birth father was a little bit sad, but he never showed it, and he never talked to me about it. I visited my birth father every Sunday. It was fun. We watched sports on TV, played sports outside, went to professional sporting events (my dad liked sports), flew kites, went on Easter egg hunts, ate lunch outside on the picnic table, and went on vacations to upper state New York where my other grandmother owned a summer cottage.

It was fun to have a stepfather too. He joined Boy Scouts with me, became an umpire in my Little League, took us to drive-in movies and out for ice cream. He even let me cut the grass on the riding lawn mower. I felt great having two dads.

Then my dad decided to get married. I was eighteen years old, getting ready to go away to college. He found a wonderful lady at work whom he liked and wanted to spend a lot of time with. I was a little bit jealous. The times that he would spend with me she would be with us. I missed the times that we would spend time together alone—just me and my dad. I liked my dad's girlfriend very much, but for the first time I started feeling sad and angry that my parents had gotten a divorce. I even cried for the first time over the fact that I didn't have a normal two-parent family. Why did all this have to happen to me? Why did my parents make believe that there was no pain? I sure felt it now! I wasn't mad at my dad, I was just feeling everything then that I should have felt back when I was five years old. I felt lousy.

> *I missed the times that we would spend time together alone—just me and my dad.*

I went on a canoe trip to Canada with our high-school football team the summer before my senior year. One of the requirements of the trip was to complete a twenty-four-hour solo. This meant that we would spend twenty-four hours on part of the island camping alone. I thought that it would be easy. Early in the morning, they dropped me off on the north side of the big island. They gave me a can of stew and a book of matches and said, "See you tomorrow." I quickly found my campsite on top of the ridge and built a fire. Then I went on a hike through the woods. I started to get hungry, so I opened my can of stew with a sharp rock down by the beach and lit my fire. After dinner, I got sort of bored and lonely. I began to think that this twenty-four hours was going to be a pretty long time without someone to talk to.

> *I started to get hungry, so I opened my can of stew with a sharp rock down by the beach and lit my fire. After dinner, I got sort of bored and lonely.*

It was at that moment that I met my third dad—my heavenly Father. He came along just at the right time. He listened to me and gave me guidance. He seemed to know how I felt about my parents' divorce. He allowed me to feel the pain of having two dads and then gave me comfort to help ease the pain. He loved me unconditionally. It was so good to be able to talk to someone. I realized at that moment that God was with me and that He was always with me. It was so exciting to finally have a dad that I could talk to all the time. I didn't have to wait until Sunday to see Him. I didn't have to wait until He came home from working his second job to talk to Him. I could pray and talk to Him any time.

> *It was so good to be able to talk to someone.*

God helped me by giving me strength when I was weak, by promising never to leave me when I was afraid, by forgiving my sin so I could forgive my parents' sin, and by giving me peace and love through Jesus Christ. God can comfort you too. You matter to God, and He would love to adopt you into His wonderful family. No matter how many dads you have, God would love to be your heavenly Father. Just ask Him, and He will do it!

WHAT THE BIBLE SAYS

Get rid of all bitterness, rage and anger, brawling and slander, along with every form of malice. Be kind and compassionate to one another, forgiving each other, just as in Christ God forgave you. (Eph. 4:31–32 NIV)

Have you forgiven your parents for the divorce? _____

What other things do you need to forgive them for? _____

_____

_____

In what ways are you not forgiving your parents? _____

_____

_____

In what ways has God forgiven you? _____

_____

_____

In what areas of your life do you need God's forgiveness right now?

_____

_____

My Personal Journal

Forgiveness

```
C M C O X K X D G Z J A Y Q V
Y W C K N S W F I G H T S M W
B N K Z E A Q T R D B H C O S
P P Y A G T W A L I E V V N D
Y Z V I L W L K F R I B W E G
B F W H E D J F R E N S F Y Z
B O Z U C M R X I M G A D L V
O R K R T W F L E A D D I N G
Y G E T B K J U N R U N V O M
F E B A D M O O D R M E O T R
R T U T O W X H I I B S R T N
I T Z P E M C F P A T S C H O
E I D M O V I N G G B B E E B
N N D W S W X K D E L N O R K
D G X L B U N F A I R T R E L
```

Find the following words in the puzzle above. They are hidden vertically and horizontally.

BADMOOD	BEINGDUMB	BOYFRIEND	DIVORCE
FIGHTS	FORGETTING	GIRLFRIEND	HURT
MONEY	MOVING	NEGLECT	NOTTHERE
REMARRIAGE	SADNESS	UNFAIR	

Where Is God When I Hurt?

In this section we will ask the question, "Where is God when I hurt?" We will begin by looking at what the Bible says about suffering and comfort. God has promised to comfort us when we feel bad, but He has not promised to take away the pain on earth. God said in Revelation 21:3, 4 that when we get to heaven He will wipe every tear from our eyes. In heaven there will be no more death, divorce, separation, grief, crying, or pain.

The purpose of this section is for you to see two things:

▶ Jesus wants to comfort your hurt. By hearing what other kids say, you will know you are not alone.

▶ Jesus wants to forgive your sin. You matter to God. He wants to be your heavenly Father by adopting you into His family.

We hope when you are finished with this section you will be able to answer the question, Where is God when I hurt?

Action Steps for Chapter 11

GOAL FOR THE CHILD
- To understand the difference between physical and emotional pain

OBJECTIVES FOR THE CHILD
- To talk about physical pain
- To talk about emotional pain
- To ask questions about relationships
- To ask the question, Where is God when I hurt?
- To ask the question, Can God really heal my hurt?
- To begin to learn about suffering
- To begin to learn about comfort

STEPS
- Facilitator or child reads quotes at beginning of chapter
- Child answers questions about relationships
- Facilitator and child discuss the answers to questions
- Facilitator and child discuss the emotional hurts of the child

IDEAS
- Encourage the child to identify the emotional pain in his life and ask the question, Will the hurt ever stop?
- Encourage the child to identify ways that God can begin to heal that hurt.
- Ask the child to draw the pain or to write about it in a journal exercise if he is unable to talk about the emotional pain.
- Do not try to answer all of the questions with ''pat'' answers. It is okay to leave some questions unanswered. The goal is not to have an answer for every question, but to begin to ask the questions about painful issues. Healing will come about more from asking questions than from gathering up quick and easy answers.
- Make appropriate referrals when needed. Do not be afraid to involve the help of a qualified, trained professional when reactions seem severe.

Chapter 11

Hurts Band-Aids Can't Cover

Many people ask the question: "Where is God when I hurt?" Here are some young persons' answers to that question.

He is always with me.

Right beside me.

God is always there when we hurt.

He's always with you.

He is always here.

Deep in my heart.

In your heart.

God is in heaven. I can pray to Him, and He will hear me.

In heaven.

He is in my heart trying to work things out.

God is in my heart when I'm hurt. He is helpful to me. He's always there when I need Him.

Make It Your Own

 What is the main reason people marry?

_____

_____

_____

What is the main reason people divorce?

_____

_____

_____

_____

What is the most important thing to look for in a husband/wife?

_____

_____

_____

_____

What is the most important thing to look for in a boy/girlfriend?

_____

_____

_____

_____

How will your parents' divorce affect your marriage?

_____

_____

_____

_____

Why does God allow divorce to happen?

_____

_____

_____

_____

What can God do to heal broken relationships?

_____

_____

_____

_____

Is it better to live in a family where there is a lot of fighting and conflict, or is it better to live in a divorced family? Why?

_____

_____

_____

_____

What are some of the positive results of your parents' divorce?

_____

_____

_____

_____

What has God taught you through your parents' divorce?

_____

_____

_____

_____

Action Steps for Chapter 12

GOAL FOR THE CHILD
- To understand what God says about suffering

OBJECTIVES FOR THE CHILD
- To learn about trouble
- To learn about patience
- To learn about character
- To learn about hope
- To talk about the suffering in your life

STEPS
- Facilitator or child reads the Bible passage about suffering
- Child draws a picture about the suffering in her life
- Child explains the drawing to facilitator
- Facilitator or child reads definitions
- Child answers questions
- Facilitator and child discuss the four stages of suffering: trouble, patience, character, hope

IDEAS
- Use the words *suffering* and *trouble* to mean the same thing.
- Be aware of the child who moves away from trouble too fast; she is really avoiding the issues brought about by the trouble.
- Be aware also of the child who is stuck in the first stage of trouble and refuses to move ahead to patience, character, and hope; she believes that nothing good can come out of a bad situation.
- Explain to the child how trouble can change into patience, then character, then hope; much like a caterpillar changes into a cocoon and then into a beautiful butterfly.
- Define hope to the child as God's comfort to help ease the pain. This definition helps to tie Chapter 12 in with Chapter 13.

What the Bible Says About Suffering

We have been made right with God because of our faith. So we have peace with God through our Lord Jesus Christ. Through our faith, Christ has brought us into that blessing of God's grace that we now enjoy.

And we are happy because of the hope we have of sharing God's glory. And we also have joy with our troubles because we know that these troubles produce patience. And patience produces character, and character produces hope.

And this hope will never disappoint us, because God has poured out His love to fill our hearts. God gave us His love through the Holy Spirit, whom God has given to us. (Rom. 5:1–5 NCV)

Draw a picture that shows the suffering in your life.

TROUBLE, PATIENCE, CHARACTER, AND HOPE

▶ The dictionary defines **trouble** as a disturbance or distress.

When there is trouble in our lives, it is upsetting. The Bible says to have joy with our troubles, because better things are on their way. It is up to you to tell God how you feel about these troubles so that He can help you feel better about them.

The Bible says to have joy with our troubles, because better things are on their way.

▶ The dictionary defines **patience** as bearing pain without complaint.

The reason we should have joy with our troubles is because these troubles produce patience. The hardest part is having to wait for something good to happen. It is like waiting in line for a ride at the amusement park or waiting until after dinner to eat ice cream for dessert.

> *The hardest part is having to wait for something good to happen.*

▶ The dictionary defines **character** as personal features or good qualities.

The reason that patience turns into character is because you develop personal qualities while you wait. Anybody can be impatient and get tired of waiting, but only those people who know how to be patient will develop character. Another way to look at character is "who you are when nobody is looking." It is easy to look good in front of your friends, but what you do at home when your friends are not around tells a great deal about your character. Try to let God shape your character.

> *Another way to look at character is "who you are when nobody is looking."*

▶ The dictionary defines **hope** as expecting with desire.

Hope comes when we long for something and expect that it will happen. It is a step above patience. We need to allow trouble to produce patience, and patience to produce character, and character to produce hope so that we will long for and expect the good to come. Life has no guarantees. Trouble will come, but if it produces hope, then it will not defeat us. Hope will also lead us to faith, which is "being sure of what we hope for and certain of what we do not see." (See Heb. 11:1.)

> *Life has no guarantees. Trouble will come, but if it produces hope, then it will not defeat us.*

Make It Your Own

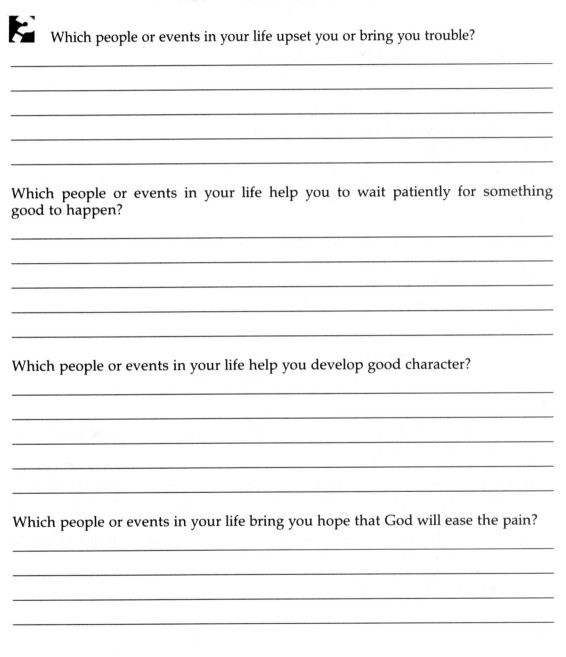

Which people or events in your life upset you or bring you trouble?

_____

_____

_____

_____

_____

Which people or events in your life help you to wait patiently for something good to happen?

_____

_____

_____

_____

_____

Which people or events in your life help you develop good character?

_____

_____

_____

_____

_____

Which people or events in your life bring you hope that God will ease the pain?

_____

_____

_____

_____

Action Steps for Chapter 13

GOAL FOR THE CHILD
- To understand what God says about comfort

OBJECTIVES FOR THE CHILD
- To talk about the comfort in your life
- To read how God has comforted other people
- To write a letter to God
- To learn how God uses suffering and comfort together
- To learn how to comfort other people with the same comfort we receive from God

STEPS
- Facilitator or child reads the Bible passage about comfort
- Child draws a picture about the comfort in his life
- Child explains the drawing to you
- Facilitator or child reads letters to God
- Child writes own letter to God
- Facilitator or child reads the Bible verse
- Child answers the questions and writes in journal
- Child finds suffering and comfort in the word search puzzle

IDEAS
- Start where you left off in Chapter 12; define hope to the child as God's comfort to help ease the pain.
- Help the child understand how God uses suffering and comfort together; God never promised to protect us from painful situations or to take away the pain. He gives us comfort to help with the pain but doesn't take away all the pain until we get to heaven.
- Explain to the child that comfort is like a flu virus—God meant for us to catch it and pass it along to others: We call this the "comfort virus."
- Explain to the child that not only will God give comfort, but that he matters to God. God wants to be his Father and adopt him into His family.

Chapter 13

What the Bible Says About Comfort

Praise be to the God and Father of our Lord Jesus Christ. God is the Father who is full of mercy. And he is the God of all comfort. He comforts us every time we have trouble, so that we can comfort others when they have trouble. We can comfort them with the same comfort that God gives us.

We share in the many sufferings of Christ. In the same way, much comfort comes to us through Christ.

If we have troubles, it is for your comfort and salvation. If we have comfort, then you also have comfort. This helps you to accept patiently the same sufferings that we have.

Our hope for you is strong. We know that you share in our sufferings. So we know that you also share in the comfort we receive. (2 Cor. 1:3–7 NCV)

Draw a cartoon or picture that shows the comfort in your life.

Letters to God

Dear God,

I want a new dad.

Please forgive all the sins I have committed. I love you very much, and some day I hope I will visit you.

How are you? How are all my friends in heaven? How's Granny? Thank you for being with me when I needed you. You're the only one I can be with forever. I can't wait until Easter! Easter is when I think about Jesus' dying on the cross.

I feel you can help me. I love you.

I love you God, so much!

My family is going through a crisis. I love both of my parents. I've never hated them. But please forgive me for all my sins. Help my parents—please!

Help me to do good in my soccer game. Help my family to be happy. Help me not to be upset when the baby-sitter comes.

I feel real sad about my parents' separating. Can you please help me?

Thank you for the things you have done and given us.

I love you, and I always will.

I guess this is for the best. This is working out very good!

Thank you for helping me for these long five and a half years when my mom and dad were divorced. I wish they could get back together, but I guess they can't.

I thank you. When my dad left, you really made me feel good. I knew you were with me all the time. I just want to say thank you. I love you, God.

I love you God. Thank you for saving us from our sins and dying for us, God. I love you.

I'm thankful that you are in my heart. I'm glad that you are always there.

Hello, I just wanted to say that I love you, and I'm glad you are in my heart. I can't wait till I see you up in heaven. Well, I love you and thank you for loving me.

I have not been saying my prayers every day. Why did you have to die on the cross? I want to go to heaven; I don't want to go to hell—not at all.

I have two questions for you: What is it like in heaven, and do you look like you did when you died?

Thank you for dying on the cross and taking away our sins. Help my mom get out of jail.

Thank you for dying on the cross.

Thank you for making me better.

I am sad because my dad died in a car accident when I was four. I am mad that I have to write the letter because I don't want to.

Hi! Are my brother and cousin up there? Do you age in heaven? Is my brother older? If I die at age ninety, would I stay that age?

This week I learned a lot about you and parents. We just got done with a session. I am glad I came. I feel great. We sang songs; that was fun. I just want to thank you for keeping me safe and letting me have fun. This has been a great week.

The thing that bugs me most is that I don't get to see my dad.

I'm glad that I've been saved and that you've come into my heart. Now I want to thank you for helping my dad get the money to send me to camp. Now that you've come into my heart, I've moved closer to you. I've always wanted to write a letter to you, but my sister comes in my room or I forget. Lord, once again, please forgive me for my sins. In your holy name, Amen.

I love you. How are you? How is my mom?

Hi! Thanks a lot for giving my mom money to send us here. I really am having fun. At camp I learned new songs, and here in the mornings we have a meeting, and I found out why I'm feeling like I am. Well, that's all.

I hope you take me to heaven and love me for whatever I do. I know you will. I had a great time at camp this week. I thank you for the rain and sun and for the great people I shared my week with. Thanks God, I love you.

What bugs me most about my parents' separation is that my dad lives with his girlfriend.

The thing that bugs me most is when my mom and dad fight.

The thing that bugs me the most is when my mom comes home from work and does not pay attention to me.

Make It Your Own

Write a letter to God. Tell Him how you feel about the separation, the divorce, the hurt in your life, His comfort in your life, and your relationship with Him.

Dear God,

_____

_____

_____

_____

_____

_____

_____

_____

_____

_____

_____

_____

_____

_____

_____

_____

_____

_____

_____

_____

WHAT THE BIBLE SAYS

These things I have spoken to you, that in Me you may have peace. In the world you have tribulation, but take courage; I have overcome the world. (John 16:33 NAS)

Make It Your Own

Is there trouble in your life? _____

In what ways has God helped you with your trouble? _____
_____
_____

In what ways are you refusing to let God help you? _____
_____
_____

Do you need to reach out to Jesus and hold on tight right now? _____

My Personal Journal

_____
_____
_____
_____
_____
_____
_____
_____
_____
_____
_____
_____
_____
_____
_____
_____

_____

_____

_____

Romans 5:1–5

```
A P C P O U R E D K X L D Q P
K N H A P P Y W G R R J I P A
N S Q B W E L P Q I V H S E T
O T U L K N X B T G G V A L I
W J J E B F E W R H L A P D E
M Z Z S H A H C O T O D P J N
Z L A S O I P O U F R Z O O C
K F A I P T H M B Q Y Q I Y E
J J X N E H B I L W G V N H Q
W P Q G P M V U E F X C T F D
J E E E P Q U G S X L T K N W
A A V L J F I L L J I K D Z D
S C L O V E C H A R A C T E R
S E L H E A R T S T U W S E T
I S P I R I T A Y S D Y T A F
```

Find the following words in the puzzle above. They are hidden vertically and horizontally.

BLESSING	CHARACTER	DISAPPOINT	FAITH
FILL	GLORY	HAPPY	HEARTS
HOPE	JOY	KNOW	LOVE
PATIENCE	PEACE	POURED	RIGHT
SPIRIT	TROUBLES		

Family Secrets

This section explores topics that are not mentioned often. Maybe that is why people call them "Family Secrets."

We will talk about adultery, abuse, and addiction. We will look at what the dictionary, the Bible, counselors, and kids like you say about these topics.

We will learn about families that don't work very well because they have rules like: don't talk, don't feel, and don't trust.

Finally, we see how someone living in a family like this can break the cycle of family secrets.

Action Steps for Chapter 14

GOAL FOR THE CHILD
- To understand the truth about adultery

OBJECTIVES FOR THE CHILD
- To learn what kids like you say adultery is
- To learn how the dictionary defines adultery
- To learn what counselors say about adultery
- To learn what the Bible says about adultery
- To write down your own thoughts about adultery

STEPS
- Facilitator or child reads what the dictionary says
- Facilitator or child reads what counselors say
- Child checks what she thinks adultery is
- Child writes out own definition of adultery
- Facilitator discusses with child her definition of adultery
- Facilitator or child reads what the Bible says
- Child rewrites own definition of adultery
- Facilitator discusses with child the difference between the two definitions

IDEAS
- Define adultery for small children as "mommy/daddy is pretending to be married to someone else."
- Describe only the behavior of the parent; do not add emotional editorials. This can force the child into taking sides.
- Stress that the importance of children's knowing the truth about adultery lies in the idea that kids think that the divorce was their fault unless they are told otherwise.
- Try to enlighten the person who committed adultery to the fact that their children will find out sooner or later. If they are not told by their parents, they will lose trust in them and wonder how many other things their parents have lied to them about. Honesty is best. Adultery is not an adult issue; it is a family concern. *When* a child is told and *how* a child is told are the two variables, not *if* the child should be told.
- Try to preserve the relationship between the child and the parent who committed adultery. Forgiveness is necessary in the process.

Chapter 14

What Is Adultery?

▶ The dictionary defines adultery as voluntary sexual intercourse between a married man and someone other than his wife, or between a married woman and someone other than her husband.

Counselors say that adultery is pretending to be married to someone else. It is when your mother or father pretends that he or she is married to another person. He or she does things with that person that should only be done with a husband or wife. Sometimes adults call adultery "having an affair." They don't want it to sound like something bad has happened. But something bad did happen. It's called "adultery." And that's a problem that can hurt a lot of people.

> *Sometimes adults call adultery "having an affair." They don't want it to sound like something bad has happened. But something bad did happen.*

Make It Your Own

Which of the following defines adultery for you?
- ☐ Going to the movies with someone other than wife/husband
- ☐ Going out on a date with someone other than wife/husband
- ☐ Going out to dinner with someone other than wife/husband
- ☐ Having a boyfriend/girlfriend
- ☐ Sleeping over at his or her house
- ☐ Living with someone other than wife/husband
- ☐ Having an affair
- ☐ Kissing someone other than wife/husband
- ☐ Sleeping with them
- ☐ Having a fight with your wife/husband

☐ Leaving your family

☐ Taking your secretary out to lunch

What do you say adultery is?

_____

_____

_____

_____

_____

_____

_____

_____

_____

WHAT THE BIBLE SAYS ABOUT ADULTERY

But when God made the world, He made them male and female. So a man will leave his father and mother and be united with his wife. And the two people will become one body. So the people are not two, but one. God has joined the two people together. So no one should separate them. (Mark 10:6–9 NCV)

Marriage should be honored by everyone. Husband and wife should keep their marriage pure. God will judge guilty those who take part in sexual sins. (Heb. 13:4 NCV)

You must not be guilty of adultery. (Ex. 20:14 NCV)

A man who takes part in adultery doesn't have any sense. He will destroy himself. He will be beaten up and disgraced. And his shame will never go away. (Prov. 6:32–33 NCV)

Make It Your Own

 What do you say adultery is now?

_____

_____

_____

Action Steps for Chapter 15

GOAL FOR THE CHILD
- To understand the truth about abuse

OBJECTIVES FOR THE CHILD
- To learn what kids like you say abuse is
- To learn how the dictionary defines abuse
- To learn what counselors say about abuse
- To learn what the Bible says about abuse
- To write down your own thoughts about abuse

STEPS
- Facilitator or child reads what the dictionary says
- Facilitator or child reads what counselors say
- Child checks what he thinks abuse is
- Child writes out own definition of abuse
- Facilitator discusses with child his definition of abuse
- Facilitator or child reads what the Bible says
- Child rewrites own definition of abuse
- Facilitator discusses with child the difference between the two definitions

IDEAS
- Be thorough when discussing the four types of abuse outlined under "what counselors say about abuse."
- Have the child describe the types of abuse he has seen in his family or in someone else's family.
- Explain to the child that if his safety is in danger, he must tell someone for his own protection.
- Explain to the child that the abuser in his family needs help. People are trained to help those who abuse others.
- Call the abuse hot line in your area if you feel that the child's safety is in danger. Your identity will remain anonymous. You can find the number in the yellow pages under human resources in your community or call your local police department. Do not be afraid to refer a harmful situation to professionals trained to handle abuse.

Chapter 15

What Is Abuse?

The dictionary defines abuse as

▶ Improper use or treatment

▶ Abusive language

▶ Physical maltreatment

▶ Expressing condemnation or disapproval

Counselors say that abuse is things that are done by one person that deeply hurt another person. Abuse can fall into many categories.

FOUR MAIN FORMS OF ABUSE

▶ **Verbal.** Something is said by someone to another that is very mean. It is not an attack on someone's behavior, but on the person himself. It is not only yelling at persons for what they have done, but also making them feel bad about who they are.

> *It is not only yelling at persons for what they have done, but also making them feel bad about who they are.*

▶ **Emotional.** Something is done to you that damages your emotions for a long time like when people pick on you and make you feel bad about yourself. Emotional abuse is usually connected with other forms of abuse.

▶ **Physical.** Somebody hurts your body. When you are hit for no reason, punished physically by someone out of anger, or have bruises from the punishment that you have received, you are being physically abused. Some adults confuse discipline with abuse. If you are unsure, talk to a counselor or teacher.

> *Some adults confuse discipline with abuse. If you are unsure, talk to a counselor or teacher.*

▶ **Sexual.** Someone touches you in a place on your body where you do not want to be touched. It also might include someone's asking you to touch him in a place on his body that you do not want to touch. It is wrong for people to do this! It is not normal and needs to be stopped. If they tell you that it is a secret and not to tell anyone, *do not listen to them!* If they tell you that they will hurt you if you tell someone, *do not believe them!* You must tell a counselor, a teacher, or your parents about this type of abuse, if it is happening to you. Only then can someone stop it.

> *If they tell you that it is a secret and not to tell anyone, do not listen to them!*

Make It Your Own

What do you think defines abuse?

- ☐ Yelling at somebody
- ☐ Hurting somebody's feelings
- ☐ Taking somebody's things
- ☐ Calling somebody names
- ☐ Throwing things at people
- ☐ Hitting someone
- ☐ Touching someone where you shouldn't
- ☐ Going to bed without eating dinner
- ☐ Going to school without eating breakfast
- ☐ Coming home from school to an empty house
- ☐ Kicking someone
- ☐ Telling someone how you feel about them

What do you say abuse is?

_____

_____

_____

_____

WHAT THE BIBLE SAYS ABOUT ABUSE

But now you also, put them all aside: anger, wrath, malice, slander, and abusive speech from your mouth.   (Col. 3:8 NAS)

Let no unwholesome word proceed from your mouth, but only such a word as is good for edification according to the need of the moment, that it may give grace to those who hear.   (Eph. 4:29 NAS)

Let all bitterness and wrath and anger and clamor and slander be put away from you, along with all malice. And be kind to one another, tender-hearted, forgiving each other, just as God in Christ also has forgiven you.   (Eph. 4:31–32 NAS)

And just as you want people to treat you, treat them in the same way.   (Luke 6:31 NAS)

Make It Your Own

What do you say abuse is now?

_____

_____

_____

_____

Action Steps for Chapter 16

GOAL FOR THE CHILD
- To understand the truth about addiction

OBJECTIVES FOR THE CHILD
- To learn what kids like you say addiction is
- To learn how the dictionary defines addiction
- To learn what counselors say about addiction
- To learn what the Bible says about addiction
- To write down your own thoughts about addiction

STEPS
- Facilitator or child reads what the dictionary says
- Facilitator or child reads what counselors say
- Child checks what she thinks addiction is
- Child writes out her own definition of addiction
- Facilitator discusses with child her definition of addiction
- Facilitator or child reads what the Bible says
- Child rewrites her definition of addiction
- Facilitator discusses with child the difference between her two definitions

IDEAS
- Be thorough when discussing the eight types of addiction outlined under "what counselors say about addiction."
- Have the child describe the types of addiction she has seen in her family or in someone else's family.
- Explain to the child that the addict needs help. People are trained to help those who are addicts.
- Avoid smoke screens about addictive behaviors such as: "What I am doing is perfectly legal, lawful, and a gray area in the Bible." People who say these things are missing the point that all things are lawful, but not all things are good for you or your children (See 1 Cor. 6:12).
- Encourage parents to take a good and hard look at the things they do that are not profitable. Explain to them that their addictive behaviors have a good chance of being passed on to their children.

Chapter 16

What Is Addiction?

The dictionary defines addiction as

▶ The practice of being harmfully attached to something

▶ Your body's dependence on something to keep it satisfied

Counselors say that addiction is things that are done by someone that hurt that person. An addiction is a behavior that controls the life of the addict and ends up destroying him. Other people close to the addict are affected also by the addiction. It is similar to abuse because the addict is abusing and hurting himself. Addictions can fall into many categories.

An addiction is a behavior that controls the life of the addict and ends up destroying him. Other people close to the addict are affected also by the addiction.

SOME POSSIBLE ADDICTIONS

▶ **Alcohol.** When a person drinks too much, doesn't remember what she did or said when drinking, or hurts others when drinking, she might have an alcohol addiction.

▶ **Drugs.** When a person takes illegal drugs or can't stop taking legal drugs like caffeine (coffee, tea, soda, chocolate), nicotine (cigarettes), or pain relievers (aspirin, Tylenol, Advil), he might have a drug addiction.

▶ **Food.** When a person eats too much, can't stop eating, only eats foods that are bad for her, is always hungry, or never eats, she might have an eating disorder or a food addiction.

▶ **Gambling.** When a person spends money on lottery tickets, betting on games, or other forms of gambling and doesn't provide for his own needs or the needs of the family, he might have a gambling addiction.

▶ **Television.** When a person spends more time sitting in front of the television than working or sleeping or can't seem to turn TV off to talk with someone, she might have a television addiction.

▶ **Possessions.** When a person has more things than he needs but thinks he needs more things and continues to buy more things, he might have an addiction to possessions.

▶ **Work.** When a person works too much, can't take her mind off work at home, works at home, never stops working, or fails to take care of the emotional needs of her family because of work, she might have a work addiction.

▶ **Religion.** When a person uses religion as an excuse to avoid God or the needs of the family and uses religion or the church as a type of work addiction, he might be addicted to religion.

Make It Your Own

What do you think defines addiction?

- ☐ Drinking alcohol
- ☐ Taking drugs
- ☐ Drinking too much coffee
- ☐ Staying at work too late
- ☐ Going to church three times a week
- ☐ Eating too much
- ☐ Buying a lottery ticket
- ☐ Buying too many clothes
- ☐ Buying too many baseball cards
- ☐ Playing too many video games
- ☐ Doing something that hurts yourself
- ☐ Doing homework too much

What do you say addiction is?

_____

_____

_____

WHAT THE BIBLE SAYS ABOUT ADDICTION

And do not get drunk with wine, for that is dissipation, but be filled with the spirit.
(Eph. 5:18 NAS)

Wine is a mocker, strong drink a brawler, And whoever is intoxicated by it is not wise.
(Prov. 20:1 NAS)

All things are lawful for me, but not all things are profitable. All things are lawful for me, but I will not be mastered by anything . . . Or do you not know that your body is a temple of the Holy Spirit who is in you, whom you have from God, and that you are not your own? (1 Cor. 6:12, 19 NAS)

Finally, brethren, whatever is true, whatever is honorable, whatever is right, whatever is pure, whatever is lovely, whatever is of good repute, if there is any excellence and if anything worthy of praise, let your mind dwell on these things. (Phil. 4:8 NAS)

Make It Your Own

What do you say addiction is now?

_____

_____

_____

Action Steps for Chapter 17

GOAL FOR THE CHILD

- To understand the truth about dysfunctional families

OBJECTIVES FOR THE CHILD

- To learn about functional families
- To learn about dysfunctional families
- To learn more about family secrets
- To learn about breaking the cycle
- To draw your family

STEPS

- Facilitator or child reads about functional/dysfunctional families
- Facilitator and child discuss what they have just read
- Child checks the concerns that he has in his family
- Facilitator discusses the items that the child checked
- Child draws his family
- Child explains drawing
- Facilitator or child reads the Bible verses
- Child answers the related questions and writes in journal
- Child finds good things in the word search puzzle

IDEAS

- Make sure the child understands the differences between functional and dysfunctional families. Explain that most families have both functional and dysfunctional characteristics: some families are more functional; other families are more dysfunctional.
- Have the child identify the functional areas of his family.
- Have the child identify the dysfunctional areas of his family.
- Have the child identify the family secrets in his family.
- Help the child learn ways to break the cycle of dysfunctional family secrets.
- Discuss with the child what God says about the family and how it should work.

Chapter 17

Breaking the Cycle

If you were riding your bike and the air in the tires started leaking out of them, it would be hard to keep going. You would have to pedal harder to keep up. It just wouldn't work very well.

If you were listening to music on your cassette tape player and the batteries started running low, it would be hard to listen to the music. The tape would start to play slower until finally the tape player would not work at all.

Our families are like that. Some work well (like a bike with tires filled with air), and some don't work very well (like a tape player with weak batteries).

Families that work well are called *functional families*. In a functional family, family members are encouraged to express their feelings. In a functional family, people feel loved, safe, and secure. Children feel cared for in functional families.

> *In a functional family, family members are encouraged to express their feelings. In a functional family, people feel loved, safe, and secure.*

Families that don't work very well are called *dysfunctional families*. A dysfunctional family has unwritten rules. Three of these rules are:

▶ **Don't talk.** Kids are told to be seen, but not heard.

▶ **Don't feel.** Kids are told that emotions are for wimps.

▶ **Don't trust.** Kids are told that you can only count on yourself.

Dysfunctional families have family secrets like adultery, abuse, and addiction. These family secrets keep the family from being healthy or working together. Family members in dysfunctional families do not feel safe, secure, or cared for.

> *Dysfunctional families have family secrets like adultery, abuse, and addiction.*

How can someone who lives in a dysfunctional family break the cycle of family secrets?

▶ If you are living in a family like this and your safety is in danger, you must **tell someone** who can protect you.

▶ The abuser or addict in your family needs to **get help.** This means that the abuse or addiction will have to stop being a secret from people who can help your family.

▶ You need to **find other kids** who have similar backgrounds to help you deal with problems through support and encouragement.

▶ You can **make a decision** today to break the cycle of divorce and dysfunction by having a healthy, functional family.

Make It Your Own

Which concerns do you have in your family?

☐ I am afraid to lose control of my feelings or my actions.

☐ I am afraid to express sadness, anger, joy, or happiness.

☐ I am afraid of conflict.

☐ I feel responsible for the needs of everyone around me.

☐ I have a hard time relaxing, letting go, or having fun.

☐ I tend to deny problems before I deal with them.

☐ I have a hard time developing close relationships.

☐ I am afraid that my parents will both leave me.

☐ I complain a lot about stomach and headaches.

☐ I am afraid of being hurt or rejected by others.

☐ I expect myself and others to do everything perfectly.

☐ I have a hard time making decisions.

☐ I am not allowed to talk about how I feel.

☐ I can't trust my parents to do things for me.

☐ I like to be around other people who are hurting.

What other concerns does your family have?

_____

_____

_____

_____

_____

_____

My Family Scene

What does your family look like now? Draw a cartoon or picture of them.

WHAT THE BIBLE SAYS

Love the Lord your God with all your heart, soul and strength. Always remember these commands I give you today. Teach them to your children.   (Deut. 6:5–7 NCV)

Children, obey your parents the way the Lord wants. This is the right thing to do. . . . Fathers, do not make your children angry, but raise them with the training and teaching of the Lord. (Eph. 6:1, 4 NCV)

Make It Your Own

Is it hard to obey your parents?_____

In what ways has God helped you obey your parents? _____

_____

_____

In what ways do your parents make you angry? _____

_____

_____

Will you be a better parent? Why or why not? _____

_____

_____

My Personal Journal

Philippians 4:8

```
G  V  H  Q  D  W  E  L  L  P  J  I  F  O  N
Y  Q  V  E  X  C  E  L  L  E  N  C  E  Y  W
C  L  L  W  X  B  N  E  P  S  A  Q  U  D  T
T  O  E  C  C  B  H  E  R  W  T  G  W  L  Z
R  R  A  B  D  Z  O  L  A  A  P  O  H  F  Z
U  C  X  T  A  F  N  W  I  L  W  O  Q  J  W
E  I  O  V  M  U  O  N  S  O  P  D  C  W  V
S  B  A  X  I  V  R  X  E  V  W  R  B  D  K
M  I  N  D  V  W  A  R  B  E  W  E  F  D  S
Z  J  T  C  A  U  B  I  K  L  O  P  P  P  O
K  C  Z  C  S  P  L  G  Y  Y  R  U  Y  G  I
J  F  R  Z  V  U  E  H  N  E  T  T  F  Q  E
G  N  S  D  W  R  P  T  I  W  H  E  H  H  V
L  U  N  P  C  E  P  V  S  B  Y  Z  L  W  I
E  C  I  Q  R  B  V  W  H  A  T  E  V  E  R
```

Find the following words in the puzzle above. They are hidden vertically and horizontally.

DWELL	EXCELLENCE	GOODREPUTE	HONORABLE
LOVELY	MIND	PRAISE	PURE
RIGHT	TRUE	WHATEVER	WORTHY

ANSWERS TO PUZZLES

Feelings

```
O L S Y T P W B H A P P Y C S
S O A M F S E K R I K C F O R
M N D K H Q S H O C K E D N G
P E A L X A Y E G N Y Z D F U
I L G A F R A I D D V H P U I
Y Y I S S P J Z E E O D S L T
G Y V C Y O U U C P E P F E T
G B N A V D V H M R Q E Y D Y
L M O R V A L E S E L L E S
A D D E A R H L Q S O E J L Y
D L R D N G Q P O S V S A K X
T R X F G N X L R E E S W I F
U V L V R Y C E X D G K K J
M Y B F Y U A S L O S T A I K
L H T B X P G S I S G V B A R
```

Changes

```
E P W P I W H H V D A T I N G
L U N P C F C H O R E S P V S
B S E P B E X F A M I L Y V B
K R C V A E M J Y Z P Z C G B
W O R K R L V I H J V V Y E C
R Y X F H I J E R Z I V N M E
H O M E F N F P D G S Q N P X
P V I I R G W A G F I U U T E
U G T P I S C P U A T E M Y R
B S I E E V B E O T S S O H U
C K M O N O T F C H R T N O S
I L E V D Z U K H E H I E U H
J C F J S K X X F R A O Y S
X J Y M O T H E R N M N D E X
S C H O O L I D Y F K S C B V
```

Forgiveness

```
C M C O X K K X D G Z J A Y Q V
Y W C K N S W F I G H T S M W
B N K Z E A Q T R D B H C O S
P P Y A G T W A L I E V V N D
Y Z V I L W L K F R I B W E G
B F W H E D J F R E N S F Y Z
B O Z U C M R X I M G A D L V
O R K R T W F L E A D D I N G
Y G E T B K J U N R U N V O M
F E B A D M O O D R M E O T R
R T U T O W X H I I B S R T N
I T Z P E M C F P A T S C H O
E I D M O V I N G G B B E B
N N D W S W X K D E L N O R K
D G X L B U N F A I R T R E L
```

Romans 5:1–5

```
A P C P O U R E D K X L D Q P
K N H A P P Y W G R R J I P A
N S Q B W E L P Q I V H S E T
O T U L K N X B T G G V A L I
W J J E B F E W R H L A P D E
M Z Z S H A H C O T O D P P J N
Z L A S O I P O U F R Z O O C
K F A I P T H M B Q Y Q I Y E
J J X N E H B I L W G V N H Q
W P Q G P M V U E F X C T F D
J E E P O Q U G S X L T K N W
A A V L J F I L L J I K D Z D
S C L O V E C H A R A C T E R
S E L H E A R T S T U W S E T
I S P I R I T A Y S D Y T A F
```